FROM KARL MARX TO JESUS CHRIST

This book is translated from the French edition *Itinéraire de Karl Marx à Jésus Christ*, published by Editions Montaigne, Paris.

FROM KARL MARX
TO JESUS CHRIST

by Ignace Lepp

SHEED & WARD · NEW YORK

Library of Congress Catalog Card Number. 57–10182

Nihil obstat:
    John R. Ready
    Censor Delegatus
28 April, 1958
Imprimatur:
    ✠ Robert F. Joyce, D.D.
    Bishop of Burlington
1 May, 1958

Manufactured in the United States of America

Contents

Introduction

I have always loved writing, and I have always written.

For some time, now, various friends have been urging me to write the story of my spiritual journey from Communism to the Church. It always seemed to me quite impossible. Nothing could be easier than to write about the things I had seen or thought: I didn't need anyone's advice about that. But the idea of making myself the subject of a book set up a whole train of objections and resistances.

A certain sense of modesty made it painful to me even to think of revealing to inquisitive eyes the most profound and hidden passages of my life. Centuries of Protestant and puritanical tradition suddenly asserted themselves with atavistic force in a sphere other than the more usual one of physical modesty.

Added to this was the fear, which I myself barely recognized, of admitting that I was growing old. A man who sets out to study his own past must, I felt, enjoy reliving it, and surely this would inevitably affect the intensity with which he lived the present. Should I not be shutting the door to any future?—using the word in the dynamic sense which Bergson gives to it: the only sense in which it has any real meaning. By writing the story of my life, should I not be giving it a static quality, a set and unchanging pattern which would deprive it of all living creativity and the endless influx of new experience?

But the main cause of my resistance was my love of truth. If only I had kept a diary from the age of fourteen or fifteen, everything would have been plain sailing: all I should have had to do was to reproduce it just as it was, or else incorporate its essentials in my narrative. But I have always been more interested in living than in watching myself live; and with the exception of one or two brief attempts I have never kept a diary. Even if I had, I wonder if I should now be able to disentangle the real thoughts, feelings and reactions recorded in it from what was written with the more or less conscious intention of giving any readers it might have a certain picture of myself. We all know that nothing could be less true than almost all the "frank" diaries ever written—Gide's heading the list.

If, then, I was to write a spiritual journal, it would mean that I should have to re-create a long-dead past. This is not to say that I have forgotten the facts and events, for I have a very good memory. But have facts and events any significance in themselves, apart from the interpretation we put on them? In any case, even if I am prepared to admit that the story of my childhood and youth may be worth telling, it is certainly not on account of any intrinsic interest in them, but simply because, and in so far as, they mark out the successive stages of my spiritual journey. The only way in which I can give my past this significance is by seeing it as a function of my present—of myself as I am now. When this past *was* my present, I was of course quite unable to grasp its significance. It goes without saying, then, that I shall relate my past as I see and understand it today; it may not even occur to me, at this point, to refer to matters which, at the time, seemed of paramount importance. If I had decided to write this book ten years ago, it would no doubt have been very different. Any objectivity it may have will not greatly differ from the objectivity of any of my writings on philosophy. If, for instance, I had to write my *L'Existence authentique* today, it would certainly not be in all respects the book that I wrote five years ago.

If, then, in spite of my hesitations and scruples, I let myself be persuaded to write my spiritual odyssey, it was because I believed that my testimony, for all its gaps and subjectivity, was *true,* and held something of universal application. Moreover, philosophical thought has shown me that the value of historical truth—whether the history is individual or collective—does not lie in the mere plain fact, but in whatever dynamic element that fact possesses—whatever meaning it has for us.

As for the material truth of the facts I am going to relate, I shall of course do my best to present them without any touching-up, just as I saw them at the time when they happened. I have, however, felt it right to suppress the names of certain places and living people, for nothing would induce me to incriminate anyone. My object in writing is not to stir up scandal or gratify idle curiosity, but simply to bear witness.

Again, the reader must not hope to find in this book any new arguments with which to refute Marxism. If I had agreed to write about my experiences as a Communist just after I had broken with the Party, my account would perhaps have been different. I was, as one always is at such times, full of bitterness and disappointment. But after I became a Christian and learnt to go to the heart of things, I came gradually to see how much I owed to my Communist past. People often ask me: "How far back do you date your conversion to the priesthood?" It is no taste for easy paradox, but simply respect for the truth, which makes me answer: "To the day when I applied for admission to the Young Communists." Indeed, but for that complete break with my whole previous life, it is very doubtful if I should ever have learnt the meaning of spiritual hunger and the thirst for the absolute.

I should like to apply to myself a distinction that Péguy was very fond of, and which I have discussed at length in *Existence authentique:* my attitude towards Communism was not that of an apostate but of a convert. An apostate's feelings towards the values he once honoured are all negative. Apostates from Christianity—especially apostate priests—talk only of the ugly and sordid side of the Church they once served. According to them, the hierarchy is composed exclusively of narrow reactionaries; all priests are money grubbers and out of step with the times; the great majority of Christians are spiritually inferior to pagans. One sometimes wonders how it is that these men, who think themselves intelligent and sometimes really are, could for years have belonged to a Church of this nature and served her with a devotion that often entailed major sacrifices. Much the same thing holds good with regard to apostates from Communism. When, for instance, one reads Kravenchko's *I Chose Freedom,* one cannot help wondering about the author. One can hardly think, if one has any capacity for thought at all, that *all* Communists are in bad faith.

Even Kravenchko tries to persuade the reader that he and a few other devoted supporters of the Communist regime were "sincere," although he and those of his kind all declare that they were blind, hoodwinked; now they *know* Communism to be absolute evil. So intelligence only dawned in them when they had given Communism up! On this showing, how much can one trust their present perspicacity?

The convert, on the other hand, denies none of the values which he once believed in and admired. Conversion is not a break with the past, but its fulfilment, its integration into a new existential synthesis better than the old. A comparison drawn from history may be instructive. The Emperor Julian and the writer Tertullian were both the personification of the apostate mentality. When Julian broke with the Christianity which he had once served with such frenzied zeal, he felt it his duty to oppose it tooth and nail, and started a ruthless persecution. Tertullian, in his early days, regarded the civilization bequeathed by pagan antiquity as the work of the devil. He insisted that Christians should throw overboard all Greek and Roman philosophy, all art and poetry which did not spring from the Gospels The Church did not endorse his views, whereupon Tertullian apostatized and harnessed all the energy which he had once used on her behalf into the work of fighting her.

Very different was the attitude of the philosopher Justin—a perfect example of the convert as opposed to the apostate. Whenever he saw a beautiful Athenian statue, whenever he read Plato or Seneca, his heart went out in gratitude to the Word of God who had given His light to all the peoples of the earth. And Justin died for his faith.

As my faith grew deeper I came to see how much it owed to my experience as a Communist. I am not, of course, claiming that it is nobler or more true than the faith of millions of Christians who have never been Marxists and whose spiritual life owes nothing to any source save Christianity. Any such claim would show an almost insane pride on my part, and there would be nothing whatever to bear it out. It would amount to saying that good needs evil—an obvious absurdity. But I am not now attempting to draw objective comparisons. God alone is able to assess objective reality. It may well be that, in His eyes, an unlettered peasant, whose spiritual life has gone no further than the monotonous daily recital of the rosary, is of far more value than the greatest theologian.

Let it be said once for all: in this book I am not trying to see things from the point of view of God. I am not writing as a theologian, but as a psychologist studying his own spiritual experience in the purely existential sphere. And, psychologically speaking, my faith is not that of an unlettered peasant, nor of a Thérèse of Lisieux, nor of the great majority of Christians, clerical and lay, whose religious life is an integral part of the family and social tradition which they have inherited and which they do their utmost to deepen and authenticate, each according to his capacity and the graces of his state.

The only faith to which I can bear existential witness is that of a man whose childhood and adolescence, and part of whose life as an adult, were spent outside all tradition and Christian influence; who served his apprenticeship to humanity in movements inspired by Marxism, and whose mind worked for years within the framework of Hegelian dialect. Even if I wanted to, it would be impossible for me to be a Christian otherwise than as an ex-Marxist. Were I to attempt it, my Christianity would be superficial: it would not go down to the deep roots of my being.

I came to see this only gradually. To begin with, I too thought that I was to bring forth the new man, the Christian, out of nothing. It took me time to see the deep meaning, which fitted my case so well, of one of the loveliest legends of the Middle Ages. The Cross of Christ, this legend tells us, was planted on the exact spot where, thousands of years earlier, Adam had been buried—illustrating the organic and metaphysical bond uniting the first man with Him who was to be the second Adam, the Saviour of mankind.

I should never have overcome my shame over the past or understood the part I was to play in the present if I had not met certain Christians of exceptional intelligence and with a profound understanding of reality—reality both specifically religious and psychological. First and foremost among them were Père de Lubac and Emmanuel Mounier. Through them I learnt, following the principles of Hegelian dialectic that I knew so well, to integrate my whole past to the new, supreme synthesis, never to be completed on this earth, which Christianity was to become for me.

The motives which led me to break with Communism had little to do with the usual theses of political anti-Communism, and I myself no longer see them in quite the same light as that which coloured them at the time. I know now that over and above the sociological and psychological factors, my "journey" was primarily a spiritual one. To an existentialist, however, the spiritual can never be abstract, a-temporal and a-spatial. Its roots strike deep into realities—tangible historical realities, economic, social, cultural, psychological. I shall have, then, to speak of the setting in which my childhood was spent, and of the various happenings which marked my youth. But I shall do so only in so far as it may seem necessary if my spiritual journey is to be understood. It is through the same necessity and within the same limits that I shall describe the political, social and economic structure of Soviet Russia. I shall not claim to have seen all sides of it, nor shall I deny that what most struck me may, objectively speaking and to other people, be of minor interest. I am not trying to draw up a balance sheet, under negative and positive headings, of Communist theory and practice. All I am setting out to do is to record my own testimony. This objective shows the limits set to the scope of my book, but I hope that it also emphasizes its authenticity.

1 *The Road to Damascus*

A SHIP MY CRADLE

The men from my part of the world, sailors and shipowners alike, all loved horses, cabarets, women—strong and violent pleasures of every kind. Only their passionate, almost biological, love of the vast wastes of the sea gave some touch of romance to their lives, whose horizon was otherwise so closely bounded.

As long as they were at sea they were sober and peaceable, but the minute their ships anchored they got drunk and seized on any pretext to start a row. Was it perhaps to make up for the months of loneliness and hard living which their long voyages forced on them, or were they trying to escape from the sense of insecurity which came over them as soon as they set foot on dry land? Even now, I should not like to have to answer the question, though I have thought about it ever since I could think at all. The sailors themselves, of course, would be the last to know the answer: they were not men to brood over speculative problems.

Our childish games were one unceasing imitation of a sailor's life. Small boats cut out of wood or bark took the place of the toy soldiers and wooden horses that other children love. And we learnt to swim as we learnt to walk.

With such a background it is not surprising that the average boy, once he reached the age of fourteen, went to sea for good. If he had any taste for learning, he would be on board only during the summer months and would spend the winter taking various courses at the merchant navy school, in the hope of one day becoming the captain of a deep-sea vessel. However rich his parents might be, people would have thought he was wriggling out of things if he started off otherwise than as a deck hand.

At that time many large ships were still under sail, and even steamers were far less stoutly built than they are today. This meant that out of ten seamen, nine were lost at sea. There was, in fact, no other form of death which the sailors respected. I shall never forget my grandfather's death, at which I was present as a child. The old sailor, who had been a shipowner in the second half of his life, felt that to die in one's bed—"like a dog," as he said scathingly—was an almost unbearable humiliation. All his brothers and four of his sons had died "honest deaths"—in other words, been lost at sea; he alone had to allow his family to look on at his last agony. Those who lived to grow old used to walk about with somewhat uncertain steps, leaning on stout, gold-knobbed sticks, as though it came hard to them to trust to the apparent solidity of the earth: a sailor's walk is easy and graceful only on a swaying deck. Their eyes, too, were always turned to the far horizons of the sea. The one subject on which they talked interminably to the swarm of small boys who followed them around was of course the sea and the distant ports where their ships had anchored.

In my family there were a good many shipowners. They too talked of ships, but ships which they had built, bought or sold, and which brought them not danger or adventure but money. I need hardly say that when I was a boy it was not they who most attracted me. I had not yet heard the word "materialist," but I could see the difference between the true sailor and the man who makes money out of the dangers of others.

The women spent their time waiting for their perpetually absent husbands and bringing up their children, almost all of whom had been born while their fathers were away. For in those days sailors only had leave, which lasted from three to six months, every two or three years. My mother, and the wives of some of the other captains, who probably had no great confidence in their husbands' faithfulness, made the most of the privileges their status gave them, and went everywhere with their husbands. And thus I came to be born, not in a nursing home but in a ship, somewhere on the Baltic. The dull roar which filled my adolescent dreams and has never quite died away was no doubt born of the lullabies sung to me by the sea, which have lingered in my unconscious.

A STRANGER ON EARTH

The unusual nature of my birthplace and the fact that for the first five years of my life I was almost always on the move no doubt account for the fact that the words "family" and "country" have never awakened the slightest affective echo in by heart. After all, however comfortable a captain's cabin may be, it is not a home. The sailors, who came from five or six different countries, made wonderful companions; it is entirely thanks to them that, from my earliest childhood, I have been able to jabber away after a fashion in several different languages; and they stored my imagination with much that has since stood me in good stead in my literary career. Yet one could not, with the best will in the world, regard them as a family. Almost every time we anchored, some of them would leave the ship and their places be taken by other men whom the mate, my father's second-in-command, signed on from the pubs in port.

Those who have only seen sailors in port have no idea of them as they really are. Coarse, quarrelsome and fond of the bottle as they are on land, the moment they are at sea they become sober, hardworking and loyal to each other.

There were about thirty of them in the structure that was my home when I was four or five—the first years of my life that I remember. They all spoilt me, after the fashion of rough, tenderhearted men, whose manners, for all their tender hearts, were not particularly polished. They stuffed me with sweets bought in port, taught me to swim, and introduced me to their various languages. As a rule, a few days in port were enough to see the end of their pay. Fortunately the "boss" had large reserves of tobacco and brandy which he would hand over on credit.

What most fascinated me was the innumerable and interminable stories which the sailors used to tell in the evenings. I can't remember one sailor who did not believe firmly in ghosts and mermaids. Even my father, who was better educated than they, was prepared to swear that when at sea he had seen strange beings that could only have been mermaids or the souls of sailors who had perished without the support of their captains' prayers. It is not surprising that my first novel, written when I was sixteen, had very little of the novel about it and was chiefly a recital of my memories from the time when I was a child sailor.

THE WORLD OF BOOKS

It was the declaration of war in 1914 and my father's call-up to the Navy (he was killed in the spring of 1916) which led my mother, my brother and myself to give up the wandering life we had led till then. Many years were to pass, and I had to go through innumerable experiences and to learn the art of introspection, before I came really to understand how deeply I had been affected by the unusual nature of my early childhood. Although I did not know it, the decisions and commitments which were to make up the texture of my life—that life which I wanted to be, and which I thought was, so entirely different from its original background—were none the less profoundly influenced by the fact that my childhood had been spent at sea, in continual voyages, and among sailors.

To my grandfather, my uncle (who was also my guardian) and my mother, it seemed a foregone conclusion that I should do what everyone else did, and join the Navy as soon as I was old enough. Nor did it ever occur to me to branch off on my own. My early education, therefore, was exactly like that of my brother and cousins. Gradually, however, everyone around me began to notice my precocious love of books, and at once started worrying over my complete lack of interest in any form of manual work, and my extreme ineptitude in everything except my studies. There was nothing for it but to send me to a more advanced school.

My mother's time was much taken up with the claims of social life, and not only she but my uncle and all my other relatives were quite without any intellectual curiosity. From the age of nine or ten I shut myself up in the magic but utterly unreal world of books. There was no one to advise me or to say what I was or was not to read, I read everything I could lay my hands on—adventure tales and detective stories, historical novels and accounts of travels. At an age when most children are reading books written especially for them, I was devouring Balzac, George Sand, Flaubert, Zola, Galsworthy, Scott, Galdos, Manzoni. Between the ages of nine and ten I was, in all probability, able to take in very little of the profound problems which these authors write about, for I knew nothing of sociological questions or adult passion. But the mere fact that I did read such books made me feel quite different from everyone around me. I naturally thought myself misunderstood, a creature from another sphere, who had strayed into the prosaic world of my family and the neighbours. I felt it my duty to look down on other people. Under the influence of my favourite authors—the Romantics—I withdrew into a lofty solitude with only books as companions. If it had not been for the moral earthquake which pulverized the soundproof walls of printed paper that I had built up around me, I should no doubt have grown up into a pedant completely cut off from all the realities of everyday life. I had, indeed no other ambition.

Of all the various social categories, the working class was the one I knew least. It was, I felt, even less worthy of my notice than the middle class—and that too I despised. As far as I remember, it was not until I was fifteen that I first went into the working-class or factory district of the town, although I had of course passed workingmen in the street. To me the word "workingmen" called up a picture of men whose clothes had none of the contrived carelessness of the bohemian's, but were merely sordid. They were of course unwashed, and their uncouth manners put them beyond the pale of all decent people.

One Sunday, when I was about fourteen or fifteen, I was out with two of my girl cousins, both older than myself, when we came on a party of young workingmen: such, at least, I took them to be, both from their clothes and, still more, from the coarse jokes they made as my cousins passed them. My cousins, who always felt themselves called upon to blush and look shocked if anything even faintly improper were said by a young man of their own class, did not deign to show the least annoyance over the "workmen's" indecent ribaldries: they belonged to a class which had no point of contact whatever with our own. It never occurred to me to wonder what there was to justify such contempt. Workingmen, as I saw it, could not help being common, dirty and drunk—drunk, too, in a way that was ten times as beastly as the drunkenness of sailors. I should have thought it inconceivable that they could take an interest in anything except "low pleasures," such as eating, drinking and making love (but not "loving," as people loved in novels).

And then I read Gorki's novel, *Mother*.

MOTHER

Not long ago, I reread *Mother*.

I felt considerable apprehension over thus rereading a book which thirty years earlier had played so great a part in determining the whole trend of my life. I need not have been afraid: *Mother* set the heartstrings of the mature man vibrating quite as strongly as it had once set those of the schoolboy who knew nothing of life or men. Once again it brought the tears to my eyes, and stirred my heart anew in sympathy with Pelagueya Vlasov and Andrey. The book is pathetic, but it has none of the grandiloquence which so puts one off when one tries to reread Rousseau, Zola or even Victor Hugo. Gorki will always be the mouthpiece of the hopes and struggles of millions of downtrodden people—not only those of Tsarist Russia at the beginning of the twentieth century, but of countless men and women alive today, or who have once lived, in every country on earth. The fact that I no longer wholly share the hopes of these men and women is relatively unimportant. Relatively unimportant, too, is the knowledge which I now have of the appalling disappointment and disillusionment which followed the experiment carried out thirty years

ago in Russia in the name of this hope. Nothing can alter the fact
that the hope itself is still great and beautiful, or that to thousands of
human beings it has been the means of transcending the drabness of
everyday life and achieving the purest possible *authenticity* of existence.

It is surely amazing that a novel should have had the power to
turn the whole life of a proud and extremely ambitious boy upside-
down. But I do not know of anything else that could have wrenched
me from the world of gross materialism in which I lived.

I had picked up *Mother* with the same lack of conscious choice
which at that time characterized all my reading. Yet it was my road
to Damascus. It was the first book I had ever read on working-class
life, which to me was quite as much an unknown quantity as the life
of Eskimos or Papuans. As I had no standard of comparison I did
not even see that what Gorki was describing was the condition of the
working class in Russia at the beginning of the twentieth century. It
was working-class life as such, without reference to time or space,
which I now believed I saw in a sudden flash of revelation.

Gorki did nothing to alter my mental picture of workingmen. Indeed, I should never have dreamed that men could be so tough, so
lacking in all delicacy of feeling, as the locksmith Michael Vlasov
and the other characters in the district which Gorki describes.

There was nothing "romantic" about their lives. Every day, in the
joyless, constricted atmosphere of this working-class neighbourhood,
the factory whistle gave its piercing summons, and sombre-faced men,
whose bodies were still tired out, came quickly out of the little gray
houses and scurried off like frightened black beetles.

In the chill morning twilight they walked through the narrow, un-
paved street to the tall stone cage that waited for them with cold as-
surance, illumining their muddy road with scores of greasy, yellow,
square eyes. The mud plashed under their feet as if in mocking com-
miseration. Hoarse exclamations of sleepy voices were heard; irritated, peevish, abusive language rent the air with malice. . . .

In the evening, when the sun was setting, and red rays languidly
glimmered upon the windows of the houses, the factory ejected its
people like burned-out ashes, and again they walked through the

streets, with black, smoke-covered faces, radiating the sticky odor of machine oil, and showing the gleam of hungry teeth. But now there was animation in their voices, and even gladness. The servitude of hard toil was over for the day. Supper awaited them at home, and respite.[1]

I should never have believed that the lives of working people were so wholly without "poetry." Had they any meaning? The working-man, when he got back from his day's work, "saw before him the delights of rest, the joys of the odorous tavern, and he was satisfied."

On holidays the workers slept until about ten o'clock. . . . When they returned from church, they ate pirogs, the Russian national pastry, and again lay down to sleep until the evening. The accumulated exhaustion of years had robbed them of their appetites, and to be able to eat they drank, long and deep, goading on their feeble stomachs with the biting, burning lash of vodka.

In a life of this kind, there was obviously no place for noble sentiments: husbands

quarreled with their wives, and often beat them, unsparing of their fists. The young people sat in the taverns, or enjoyed evening parties at one another's houses, played the accordion, sang vulgar songs devoid of beauty, danced, talked ribaldry, and drank. . . . They fell on one another for mere trifles, with the spiteful ferocity of beasts. . . .

Obviously, these workers had not learned the art of living. Any denunciation of them by the middle classes paled beside the brutal reality which Gorki describes. Yet Gorki was one of them, and all his sympathies lay with the wretched people in this slum. My own free time, which I used to spend with some of my schoolfellows in the select literary club to which I belonged, seemed sublime by comparison. We talked about art and literature, and always picked our words most carefully, even to express disagreement. Why, even the sailors' lives, which I had not quite forgotten, seemed far more "romantic." It was true that the ward-room, where twenty or thirty of them were herded together, hardly provided palatial living conditions, but at

[1] This quotation, and all others from *Mother* are taken from the English translation published by D. Appleton Century Co., 1938.

least there was none of the filth and squalor which made the district that Gorki describes so sickening. Then, most important of all, on a ship there are no half-starved children, no women old before their time. I felt that poverty and dirt were infinitely more revolting in women than in men. The only women I knew (I didn't quite look on the servants at home and in our friends' houses as "women") were always well-dressed, elegant and with a waft of delicious scent about them. The knowledge that there were other women who were entirely different seemed a real degradation of their sex.

The first pages of *Mother*, then, merely crystallized the somewhat vague ideas I had always had about "workingmen." I had never asked myself who was responsible for the existing state of affairs. I probably had some confused notion that, if workingmen were rough and dirty, got drunk and beat their wives and children, it was because they wanted to—because that was the way they were made. Hadn't I myself refused to become a sailor and stood out for a life of learning? What was there to stop them from doing something of the same sort and giving up their sordid type of existence? In fact, I saw little to criticize in my cousins' disdainful and condemnatory attitude towards the workingmen we passed in the street.

But I soon saw that Gorki's novel did not stop at describing the wretched conditions of the workers; it denounced those who were to blame. That, to me, was its real revelation. And the guilty ones were not the Vlasovs who drank and beat their wives, or the Vyesovshchikovs who lived by theft. The guilty ones were the rich and powerful—the cultured upper classes who treat the poor with scorn.

THE THIRST FOR JUSTICE

I was fifteen years old, and I had never yet questioned the justice of the world I knew. It is true that I considered myself the victim of injustice when my grandfather snatched from me some book I was reading, at a time when, according to him, I should be playing with other children or having organized games, "like all normal kids." I thought, too, that it was most unjust that I should have to learn chemistry and botany, when I "knew" that I was born to be a writer. But these were all injustices of which I myself was the victim. It had never crossed my mind that I too could be unjust. Still less had I ever given a thought to the justice or injustice of society or the world at large. I had not yet arrived at a stage of maturity at which one is really interested in anything except oneself. Men, things and the world were visible only in the light of my own narcissistic tendencies. Probably my intellectual precocity made me even more egocentric than most boys of my age.

Great was my surprise to learn from Gorki that the world ought not to be what it is, and that all the poverty and brutality in the mean streets he describes should call to our pity rather than our feelings of revulsion. I had never, until then, felt pity for human beings; only sick or ill-treated animals had seemed to me to deserve it. Gorki showed me that workmen who made themselves dead drunk and then beat their wives and children were quite unable to take an interest in any of the "values" which were the joy of our club of youthful aesthetes; that they were not to blame for the evils which consumed them or which they themselves committed. For the first time in my life I felt, thanks to Gorki, a piercing sense of solidarity with all the outcasts of the earth.

So, then, the luxuries and superfluities of some people were counterbalanced by the destitution of others. I saw now that if only the heads of factories would rest content with what was really necessary (I was fairly liberal in my interpretation of what they would think necessary) their workmen could live in comfortable houses and eat their fill every day. They would never have to work themselves into a state of stupefaction—which would mean that, instead of going off to some cabaret to try to forget their troubles, they would be able to take an interest in all that was fine and noble, just like us intellectuals.

My family, and everyone around me, seemed suddenly stained with the collective sins of the whole middle class. Later on, when I had come to know something of psychoanalysis, I saw that my unconscious had undoubtedly felt the need for this justification of my revolt against my family. Without admitting it—without knowing it, even—I had been suffering from the affective frustration of living among people who were not in the habit of showing tenderness or consideration, especially to a boy like myself, whose tastes and behaviour always ran counter to the traditions and routine of those around him. Until then, I had turned up my nose at my family and neighbours because of their common tastes and lack of culture, and because they saw nothing in the beautiful quotations from Goethe and Baudelaire that I was forever dinning into their ears. It was delightful now to learn that they were criminals, the accomplices of an unjust society—that the money they spent, the houses and boats they owned, had all been stolen from the workers. I at once had the gratifying feeling of cutting myself off from them in the name of a great and noble principle—Justice.

I don't deny that this was a somewhat oversimplified view of the world and its antagonisms—one fitted to my age and (why not admit it?) my complexes. I have no intention, anyhow, of justifying myself; my one aim is to try to relive, as authentically as possible, the emotions and reactions of long ago.

THE CALL TO BATTLE

It is not easy for me to remember today what sort of idea I had had of Communism before I read Gorki. I probably shared the prejudices of the people among whom I lived. For, however different we may think ourselves from the life around us, it sets its mark on us none the less. The Communists, then, were bloodthirsty scoundrels eaten up with envy of the decent people who had managed, through the sweat of their brow, to get a little property together. The minute they, the Communists, were strong enough, they would do just what they had done in Russia—rob everyone who owned anything and keep the loot for themselves.

I had, of course, heard of the egalitarianism of Communism; I had even read several novels-of-the-future describing the Communist world to be. I imagined it as a huge phalanstery, where people all lived together, nobody owned anything, and everyone slept in communal dormitories and had meals in collective refectories. No one's wife or children would be really his own. As far as I remember, the only thing that horrified me in this "communism" was the idea that even intellectually men were all to be equal, all alike obliged to read the same books, see the same plays, listen to the same music. Now my friends and I liked only "esoteric" poets whom the common herd could not understand. (It is true that sometimes we could not understand them ourselves, but that we would not have admitted for anything.)

I knew, of course, that the Communists had seized power in Russia, and either massacred all the "decent people" or driven them out of the country. Like everyone else, I had come across Russian refugees, taxi-drivers and waiters, who all said that they were generals, members of the Imperial Court, or, at the very least, princes. Once they got going on the horrors of the Revolution, it was quite impossible to stop them. I found out later that most of these self-styled aristocrats were ordinary middle-class people, and that the worst type of adventurer often masqueraded under the title of general or colonel. They probably believed firmly in the horrors they described —although in actual fact they could not all have seen so many. They made themselves out as the tragic victims of a barbarous revolution, both to seem interesting and to excite the pity of anyone whom they hoped somehow or other to make use of.

I had also read books describing the bands of homeless children in Communist Russia, who had turned into young criminals and attacked travellers by night, or organized raids on lonely farms. I knew, too, that such was the state of famine that people ate cats and dogs, or even their own parents and children. It was said, moreover, that immorality in the Soviet Union had reached monstrous, unimaginable, proportions: that no woman, unless she cared to risk being looked on as a counter-revolutionary, could refuse herself to anyone who wanted her: that people walked the streets stark naked—and so on. It seemed obvious, both to those who told the stories and to me who heard them, that Communism alone was to blame for all this poverty and immorality How, at my age, was I to know that the Communist regime had inherited the ruin and devastation caused by four years of world war and another four years of civil war? I did not then know that all the great upheavals of history have let loose the worst instincts of humanity. Had I been familiar with Christian terminology I should, no doubt, like many others, have regarded Communism as the triumph of antichrist, and Communists themselves as possessed by the devil.

Gorki's novel opened before me an entirely new horizon. With some astonishment I learnt that for millions of men and women, the outcasts of the earth, Communism shed a glow of hope over everything. According to him, even before it could change the social order, it would change men—such men, at least, as had made it the one object of their lives.

Mother contains no apology for Communist or socialist teaching— not even an outline of what it is. Gorki, being a great novelist, was content simply to portray a cross section of Russian working-class life. It is this very fact which gives his book its extraordinary powers of persuasion, so that the unsuspecting reader finds himself suddenly swept off his feet by it; whereas the chief reaction to the "pious" Communist novels of today, including Aragon's, is distrust.

Pavel Vlasov, one of the principal characters of *Mother,* was undoubtedly rather more intelligent than the other boys of his district, but there was nothing to suggest that his life would differ much from theirs. At fourteen, he had the courage to stand up to his drunkard of a father and refuse to let himself be thrashed. Some time later, a fortnight after his father's death, he himself came home drunk for the first time in his life and spoke to his mother with all his father's arrogance. His one wish was to be like everyone else.

Pavel tried to live like the rest. He did all a young lad should do— bought himself an accordion, a shirt with a starched front, a loud-colored necktie, overshoes and a cane. . . . He went to evening parties and learned to dance a quadrille and a polka. On Sundays he came home drunk.

But one day he had the good fortune to meet some men and women who were working "in the cause of the people," and his whole life changed. He gave up drink and no longer spoke rudely to his mother or anyone else; he stopped swearing and became serious and hard-working; all his spare time went into reading and study, for he had come to see that the worst enemy of the people was ignorance, and that if they were ever to achieve freedom and enlightenment it was here that the first blow must be struck. He took to attending secret meetings in town, distributed revolutionary booklets and papers in the factory, and organized a new Party cell which several young people living in his district joined. He became the acknowledged leader among his workmates; in fact, even the intellectual revolutionaries of the town looked up to him; then, gradually, the most respected of the older workmen came to see that he was a man who had the good of the People at heart and who didn't shrink from sacrifice for their sake. (What mystic undercurrents the word "people" takes on in the mouth of Gorki's characters!) He became an ascetic, a hero, in the People's cause; neither prison nor Siberia held any terrors for him; even death for such a cause could only be hailed with joy.

The other militant revolutionaries in the book were no less dedicated to the same work, and it made new men of them. These Andreys and Mitias could not have been so very different from the first Christian martyrs. Young Vyesovshchikov's father was a thief who spent half his life in prison; his own youth had been one succession of humiliations, and he joined the Party purely out of a sense of revolt. He was always on the lookout for trouble, insulted the police, and was quite ready to commit murder to get his own back, and, as he thought, avenge the countless humiliations of the People. Yet even he underwent a complete transformation after he had met Pavel and the other comrades; he became calm and disciplined, and ended by making good use of his natural impetuosity. For it was now no longer his own private vengeance that he was after, but the the triumph of the Cause.

But the real subject of the novel, as the title tells us, is Pavel's mother, Pelagueya Vlasov, and her "conversion." Her life too had been one long humiliation. She had been married, against her will, to a drunken brute who beat her every day: nor had it ever occurred to her to think that life might be different. After all, it was just the same for nearly all the women around her. All her life she had lived in a state of fear—fear of her husband, fear of the authorities, fear of the rich. When Pavel stopped drinking and began to behave himself, she was of course overjoyed, but as soon as she found out what he was up to, her fear returned. Was not her son rebelling against God and the Tsar, the rich and powerful, the government itself—everything, in fact, which all her life she had been taught to honour? She had always seen the people bow down before anyone with the least vestige of money or power. She was still afraid of some of Pavel's new friends, whose speech and manner showed that they did not come from the people. The first time the police searched her cottage she shook with fear.

But Pavel and, still more, his friend Andrey took the trouble to explain to her what their fight for the People stood for. She saw for herself how greatly the older workmen respected her son, and there gradually stole over her a wholly new and unaccustomed feeling: pride. She realized with amazement that she too was a human being, and marvelled at the affection lavished on her by Pavel's new companions, even those of noble birth. The one thing that distressed her was their irreligion. She could not understand how it was that such good men and women, all inspired by such deep love, did not believe in God or go to church, and spoke of priests with dislike and contempt. She herself was very religious. Almost before she was aware of it, the cause for which her son was fighting began to steal into her prayers; she felt that he and his friends, for all their unbelieving talk, were very like Christ, the Friend of the poor.

At one time, Pavel had been the only person she loved. Then, almost imperceptibly, her love began to embrace his companions and, through them, the People, for whom they fought and were persecuted. Her feeling of motherhood grew wider: her heart opened to take in the whole world. At first it had surprised her to hear Pavel and his friends speak of French, German and Italian workers as if they were all kith and kin; she was amazed at their noisy jubilation over the success of the London dock strike, their distress at the severe measures taken against the workers of some far-off country where none of them had ever set foot and of which she herself had never heard. "The People" were no longer just the folk of her own neighbourhood, but men and women all over the world whose lives were spent in hardship, toil and suffering. It was Andrey who put into words this new love which burned in the heart of every revolutionary:

You know, sometimes you have a wonderful feeling living in your heart. It seems to you that wherever you go, all men are comrades; all burn with one and the same fire; all are merry; all are good. Without words they all understand one another; and no one wants to hinder or insult the other. . . . All live in unison, but each heart sings its own song. And the songs flow like brooks into one stream, swelling into a huge river of bright joys, rolling free and wide down its course.

After the First of May demonstrations—the first which had ever taken place in her district—the mother decided to follow her son's lead. She had felt so proud at hearing him address the thousands of workers at the meeting that all fear suddenly left her. When Pavel, Andrey and the other militants were sent to prison, she felt herself urged on by an overpowering impulse; she caught up the torch that fell from their hands and vowed herself to the Cause. She developed a courage and resourcefulness that she would never have thought she had in her, assumed a disguise, and carried on the work of distributing revolutionary newspapers and pamphlets. She even shook off her religious faith, though she never ceased to admire and love Christ, the Friend of the poor. Whenever she came across men and women more ignorant than herself, especially if they were peasants ("Even the moujiks are beginning to want to hear the truth!"), she found words of passionate conviction in which to tell them of this Truth, and of those who worked for it.

Before I read *Mother*, I had never, as far as I remember, felt the need to make my life serve any useful purpose. Not that I was without idealism. I meant to do great things. My enthusiasms changed from year to year: I saw myself, according to whichever author or hero headed the list, as a great traveller, the explorer of uncharted regions, an eloquent lawyer, or a professor basking in the admiration of his students. But the object of every ambition was always myself. It never entered my head to wonder what good, if any, my explorations would do the "savages"; or how my teaching would help my students; or whether my books would be of any practical use to my readers. The only thing that mattered was that I should be famous; other people were simply the means to this, the ladder by which I should climb.

By the time I reached the last pages of *Mother*, the tears were streaming down my cheeks. How utterly empty and useless my life was, compared with the lives of these fighters for Truth! My personal ambitions, all centred on the one aim of getting me to the top, seemed petty and worthless beside the ambitions of men who had set themselves to change the face of the world, to transform mankind. I had sedulously defended my solitude, like the young aesthete I was; now I saw that my life would never have any real beauty or interest unless I took my place in the world-wide brotherhood of those who give up everything for the Truth. I already saw myself marching shoulder to shoulder with Pavel and Andrey, haranguing crowds, fighting oppression. I knew nothing of life and made no allowances for differences of place and time. Nor did it ever strike me that the terrible Tsarist police, the mere thought of whom made my blood boil as it had made Gorki's, had long since been replaced by the Cheka—compared with whom the Tsar's police had been meek little choirboys. But I must not anticipate.

I had found the mother herself intensely moving: Pavel, Andrey and the other revolutionary workers and peasants were all brave and likable. But they moved in a world entirely different from my own. The sordid squalor of their childhood, their hard, unglamorous toil in field or factory, were wholly alien and could have no charm for me. In 1924 the day of the priest worker had not dawned; it was not then as it is now, fairly common for young men of the middle class to throw in their lot with the workers out of an almost mystical love of the people. Besides, as I have said, I felt too strong a physical revulsion from manual labour—and, still more, from dirt—to want, even in imagination, to work in a factory.

Gorki's book had shown me, however, that not all the fighters for truth and the people's cause were workingmen or poor peasants. There was Natasha, for instance, the daughter of a rich merchant, whose love of the people made her give up everything and devote her life to teaching them. Sashenka, again, was of noble birth, and so was the intellectual, Nicolay Ivanovich, and his sister Sofya, who adored music. And there were doctors, professors, lawyers. . . . Vyesovshchikov, Rybin, even the mother herself, impressed me far less than these men and women, whose inherited privileges should, in the nature of things, have put them on the side of the established order. Instead, they rallied the forces of revolt, lived in poverty, and unflinchingly faced the prospect of prison or Siberia. Even the poverty of these aristocrats was beautiful to me, for it did not rule out books or music or endless discussions on abstract subjects. All this had some flavour of bohemianism, and attracted me far more than the harshness and above all the inevitability of working-class poverty. I myself had no wish to become a village teacher—in any case, there was no shortage of village teachers in France—but I could see myself very clearly in the company of Nicolay, Sashenka and the rest. They "went to the people" without losing any of the qualities that gave them their distinction. That, at least, is how I saw it in 1924. I had quite made up my mind to fight for Truth, Justice and the People, but I was far too self-centred to think for a moment of allowing the nobility and disinterestedness of my action to be overlooked. It was not only "the people" that I wanted to admire it; I was even more anxious that my "sacrifice" should be seen as such by the highly-educated, who would really be able to appreciate its sublimity. My "conversion," it will be seen, was not without a strong dash of vanity.

THE FIRST STEPS OF A NEOPHYTE

At this early stage, my "conversion" was still entirely theoretical. I had made one or two attempts to get into conversation with the servants or the men who worked for my family, but without success. The Russian workers described by Gorki showed an intense thirst for knowledge. They read books on history and science, for they were firmly convinced that the world, if it were ever to be transformed and conquered, must first be understood. The intellectuals who espoused the people's cause had no difficulty in making themselves useful; they recommended books to read, and explained the stiffer passages.

My mother's maid, too, was fond of reading. One day when she was out I went up to her room to see the sort of books she liked. I found, alas, nothing on the evolution of primitive races, nothing on political economy or biology. I hadn't time to make a closer examination of the books which, I knew, often made her cry; but the pictures on the covers told me that they were cheap little love stories. I myself had read quite a number of them, and knew very well what they were like. The members of our Poetry Club were loud in their denunciations of this sort of "servant-girl drivel," and it was regarded as "the thing" to speak of it with lofty disdain.

I decided that it was my duty as a revolutionary to undertake Louise's education. I lent her *Mother* and strongly urged her to read it. She was a good-natured girl and made no objection, but she kept it some months and then at last admitted that she hadn't found it at all interesting.

I was slightly more successful with Suzanne, who was nurse to my aunt's children, and only very little older than I. She listened, moist-eyed, as I discoursed on the books I'd read and my dreams of devoting my whole life to the revolution. Unfortunately these long conversations with Suzanne aroused the suspicions of my aunt, who reported them to my mother. Neither of them much believed in my efforts to convert the little nursemaid to class warfare. My sudden interest in her was, they thought, due to the fact that I had just reached puberty; and my aunt did not want any scandal in her house. Moral considerations didn't count for much with my mother, but she seized the opportunity given her by my supposed infatuation and poured out a stream of practical advice whose chief effect was to fill me with shame and embarrassment. My cousins' teasing was the last straw, and I had no choice but to close down my propaganda work among the maids. Besides, although I knew nothing of women, even I was beginning to see that Suzanne for her part was far more pleased by the interest shown in her by the "young gentleman" than by the revolutionary indoctrination I was trying to impart. I must have been a very poor teacher, not up to presenting my thesis in a way that could interest and be understood by a children's nurse.

My efforts to establish relations with workingmen met with no greater success. The house-painter then working for my family was said to be a Communist—a reputation he had won for himself by his somewhat arrogant manner and, still more, by his insistence on having proper pay, and being given it regularly every Saturday On one occasion I ran him to earth in a room he was repainting and did my best to engage him in a man-to-man conversation. I told him how disgraceful I thought it that my uncle should pay him so little, and that I should be entirely on his side if he went on strike. And more in the same vein. Needless to say, I made no secret of my Communist convictions and asked him to look on me as a Comrade. For some minutes he appeared to be listening with deep interest Or, perhaps, I did not see that there was less agreement than irony in the sly winks he kept giving me. At any rate, when I met him next day with one of my cousins and greeted him ostentatiously with "Good morning, Comrade," all he did was to laugh in my face; and I don't think I was mistaken in interpreting this as an insult.

The only people on whom I made any impression were my boy and girl cousins and their friends. To them I became almost overnight a Communist *par excellence*. It is true that the word "Communism," which to me meant all that was admirable, took on a purely pejorative sense when they used it. They announced that they now understood why I had never taken any interest in their games, and spent my whole time reading. When they called me a Communist they meant to insult me, but I took the word as a compliment. It was not quite so pleasant, however, to hear them assert authoritatively that the reason I had become a Communist was that too much reading had addled my brain. In a community where men of action alone were thought to have any merit, it really did seem a self-evident proposition that only the barmy could possibly prefer the pleasures of learning to the joys of action. Then, too, apart from what they regarded as my flirtations with the maids, I was rather standoffish with girls, whereas other boys of my age boasted shamelessly of their triumphs. Even this was put down to my Communism.

I had failed with the "proletariat" whom I had wanted to enlighten and been laughed at by the "bourgeoisie" whom I despised; there was nothing for it but to plunge still deeper into that world of books where no disappointments seemed to lie in wait for me. My school work took up only a small part of my time. It was novels, and, somewhat later, history which held me spellbound till late at night. The eclecticism which had characterized my earlier reading was over for a long time to come. From now onwards, what I looked for in books was anything that would strengthen my Communist faith. Gorki's novels and short stories were followed by Zola, Dickens, Jack London, Hugo's *Les Misérables,* and then Anatole France, Tolstoi, Henry Mann, Barbusse. . . . I was proud and pleased that my knowledge of foreign languages put the authors of so many different countries within my reach. There was still, of course, a good deal of eclecticism in my choice of authors, but it was an eclecticism whose main trend I myself controlled.

At about this time I set about writing my first novel—for I had not renounced my literary ambitions. I should have liked to write a novel to serve the Cause, as did the works of my favourite authors. After a few attempts, however, I had to admit that I knew nothing of working-class life except what I had read in books; Gorki, Barbusse and others like them had done what I was trying to do, and done it incomparably better. The only social community I really knew was the world of sailors. My first book, then, was *Gens de Mer.*

It was a description of life at sea—that life which is so full of charm, and yet so hard, even heroic. Even here, however, I felt it my duty to unearth evidence of the class struggle. It was more difficult than I thought. Among all my early memories I could not find one to suggest that there was any such hostility between deck hands and officers as exists between workmen and employers Their relations, at least on board, were certainly pretty rough-and-ready, but there was a great simplicity about them, and even a deep fellow feeling In the evening they all used to foregather on the bridge Only the captain's wife had the privilege of lying in a deck chair; the others, including my father, either sat or lay on the deck. There were no class distinctions, nor was there any sign of servility Some years later, it is true, when my "Marxist education" was in a more advanced state, I should have used all this as a golden opportunity to denounce "paternalism " Even at that time, my "revolutionary conscience" would never have forgiven me if I had failed to emphasize the differences of food, pay and living conditions between the "proletarian sailors" and their "exploiters." So I described the wretched, airless quarters below deck where the sailors lived and contrasted them with the officers' smart cabins. I did my best, too, to make the gibes and criticisms with which the sailors spoke of those over them sound like symptoms of class warfare, and the officers' bawlings-out were always represented as an expression of the hateful capitalistic spirit.

None of this was very convincing, and no one was more surprised than I when this fifteen-year-old effort found a publisher. It was the more astonishing in that I had not even any distinctive style of my own; any reader with his eyes open could have spotted the influence of my extensive reading on every page. I think the only part of the book that was worth anything was the innumerable stories of ghosts and mermaids which I had heard as a child from my grandfather or the sailors and retold in my "novel" with as few alterations as possible. This must have been the one thing that decided the publishers in its favour. The few critics, anyway, who did me the honour of mentioning this first book seemed to remember nothing else about it. One of them even said that the real author must have been an experienced sailor, as no boy of fifteen could possibly have known the life so well. I had not brought myself into the story at all, and nobody could have guessed that the author was a sailor before he had learnt to read or write.

CHILDHOOD WITHOUT GOD

Religion had played no part in my childhood, unless indeed one identifies it with superstition. Sailors—even officers—are intensely superstitious. I have myself seen many ceremonies carried out to give protection against the evil eye, ward off bad luck, and so on. Young though he was, my father assumed something of the manner and dignity of a high priest each time the ship left port, as he read out the strange formulas, dating back, no doubt, to long before the dawn of Christianity, and handed down by captains from father to son, which laid spells on the spirits of the deep not to harm the ship in any way during the voyage she was about to make. I always regret that it never occurred to me when I was young to copy out these esoteric formulas; it would be interesting now to trace them back to their source. But at the time when I could have done it, I was far too contemptuous of such "rubbishy superstitions" to take any interest in them. I have not, however, forgotten how the sailors took off their caps and listened, in an absolutely religious silence, while the captain read aloud the mysterious words of protection.

My family was Protestant: on my father's side, it had been so for centuries; on my mother's, from the beginning of the nineteenth century. Except for my maternal grandmother, whose narrow bigotry I can still remember, none of the family seemed to take religion very seriously. I don't know who first taught me, when I was very small, to say the Our Father; by the time I was an adolescent, I had forgotten even that. If I am not mistaken, my family still got married in the Protestant Church, for I remember going to several weddings there. The pastor was called in, too, to christen babies, but I could not say what rites he used. The most important thing of all, however, was that there should be a minister to officiate at every funeral. Apart from this, the supernatural played no part in the life of any of my family, though they would have felt greatly insulted if anyone had dared to suggest that they were not Christians.

The few hazy ideas on religion that I had when I was about fifteen were also picked up from novels. I had been deeply moved by the way the mother and certain other characters in Gorki spoke of religious faith, and, especially, of Christ. It was to tell the poor of God's love that Rybin gave up everything and went off to teach the truth to the peasants. Pelagueya, the mother, spoke of her son and his companions as if they were the heralds of a new God. In Tolstoi, Nekrassov and the other Russian authors whose works I pored over at this time, there were constant traces of the same mysticism, and it never failed to move me.

Yet I couldn't help noticing that these authors, who wrote so tenderly of simple, sincere Christians, were terribly severe whenever it came to any mention of Churches and priests. Priests, indeed, were always made out to be the worst enemies of the people, the stoutest supporters of that policy of oppression and injustice which all the noblest members of the working class hoped to overthrow. Then, too, they were violently opposed to any glimmer of learning's reaching the people. As I had no personal knowledge of the matter whatever, it is hardly surprising that I accepted in trust whatever these authors liked to tell me.

What, however, affected my later development more than anything was the discovery that in these spellbinding books—Tolstoi's alone excepted—the educated revolutionaries and the workers fighting for their freedom were all alike atheists. Christ, to them, was no more than a wonderful man whose personality the priests had got hold of and distorted, and whose teaching of pure love they had twisted out of recognition. The churchmen were quite clearly in bad faith, bribed by the enemies of the people to keep the rank and file submissive to the established order by lies and threats of hell-fire. I had no qualms over adopting this view without giving it a moment's independent thought. I too, I announced, was a freethinker and atheist—which of course had the pleasing result of shocking my family still further. I soon found out, of course, that the French and German socialists were avowed materialists and rationalists, without any of the halo of mysticism which I had seen over the heads of the Russians.

I made it a point of honour to run down religion and religious people as much as I possibly could, both to my family and to the boys at school. I seized every opportunity of announcing my faith in "science." If anyone had taken the trouble to probe at all deeply into my scientific concepts of the world, it wouldn't have taken him long to find out that they were no better founded nor more enlightening than the so-called Christian principles which most of my interlocutors prided themselves on. With an arrogance that ruled out all doubts and contradictions, I announced that there was no God, that men were descended from monkeys, that creation had never taken place, and that evolution explained everything. I needn't add that I couldn't have brought a single argument to bear in support of these assertions. All I had done was to make a blind act of faith and then swallow, hook, line and sinker, everything that I believed to be "Communist." I would no more have allowed any questioning of my convictions than would the most fanatical believer in God. To me it was self-evident that atheism and its postulates were "scientific"; and at that stage of my development "science" and "truth" were synonymous.

And yet I had never felt myself in the least drawn to the study of science. Literature, history, geography, languages—above all, philosophy, though that came later—all interested me far more than chemistry, botany or physics. Yet, to come into line with my idea of the perfect Marxist, I felt it my duty to read books on almost every scientific discipline that exists, hoping to find in them some argument in support of my new concept of the world My efforts were not very rewarding, and more often than not I had to make do with those little books in which science is explained to the masses in a simplified way.

Every now and then I used to buy and read Communist newspapers. Although I never dared to admit it even to myself, I didn't find them very interesting. Trivial details of working-class conditions and comments on the politics of the day were far less comprehensible to me than great ideas or noble feelings. I had not yet learnt to see the importance of a parliamentary debate on road transport, or a strike in some mine or other. I was interested in nothing but the "Great Day." Unfortunately, I knew no one capable of making me see that what, quite unconsciously, I was looking for in Communism was a faith, an ideal which would give me some good reason for living. I did not know that I belonged to that class of human beings for whom life has no value until they have found something worthy, in their eyes, to demand its sacrifice. My education, both in the family and at school, had set no ideal before me. After I had read Gorki's *Mother,* I felt that in Communism I had found that Absolute which I needed more than food or drink.

When I look back today, I don't find it easy to recapture the features of "Communism" as I saw it in the autumn of 1924 Of Marx I knew only the name. Lenin had died in January; of him I had heard slightly more, and had even brought myself to read one of his shorter works. I had an unbounded admiration for him—chiefly because he was the bugbear of the middle class. For at that time my Communism contained far more of hatred of the middle class than love of the proletariat, with whom I had not yet succeeded in getting into touch. I myself had been born into all the privileges of the middle classes, but as yet I had no direct knowledge of the social injustices of capitalism which I claimed to be fighting. What I was still particularly touchy about was the injustices—in no sense social—of which I felt I was the victim. To a very great extent what I was rebelling against was my family's lack of understanding and the teasing to which they subjected each new enthusiasm, each successive utopia, of my own. But as yet I knew nothing of such psychological explanations, and was quite unaware that in my revolt against the social order there was an admixture of purely personal revolt against my family, which accepted this order without a qualm, and found it good.

I was later to have countless opportunities of seeing that, whereas Communists from the working classes aim first and foremost at creating a new world, and regard the destruction of the old merely as an indispensable preliminary to this, Communists from the middle or upper classes approach the question from an entirely different angle. To them, what matters most is the destruction of the old world to which they once belonged and which they destroyed in their own hearts when they became Communists. Their wish to build a new world on the ruins of the old is often no more than an unconscious justification of their will for destruction, whose negative brutality they have never dared to face. They are not so much revolutionaries as men in revolt—psychological anarchists rather than Communists. Yet they have some distinguished forerunners, headed by Marx and Lenin.

These unconscious psychological motives do not, of course, lessen the human value of the enthusiasm with which I myself, and many another Communist intellectual, served our ideal.

2 *The Young Communists*

For some months after my "conversion" to Communism, I continued to be a lone Communist; my states of revolt and exaltation took place in solitude. But from the very beginning I had made up my mind to join the Party. Time and again I stood outside its headquarters, not daring to go in Probably my unconscious had not yet shaken off the impressions which made up the picture of Communism generally accepted among the people I knew. The Communist stronghold had something alarming about it, like Ali Baba's cave.

It may have been a particularly violent argument with my uncle that decided me, or perhaps I had just read something unusually inspiring. Whatever it was, one October day in 1924 I determined to cross the Party threshold. The man in charge, by way of asking what I wanted, just raised his head. "I want to join the Communist Party," I stammered. Then I suddenly realized that I'd said "Sir," and this added terribly to my confusion, for I knew from all the novels I'd read that the disciples of Marx and Lenin call each other "Comrade." But the man didn't seem to have noticed my howler, or possibly he had less regard for the conventions—even Communist conventions—than I had. He looked at me more closely, stared at my bare legs (I only wore long trousers on special occasions), and then, without taking the cigarette end from his mouth, asked, "How old are you?" I announced my fifteen years and was told that this was not nearly old enough to become a Party member. Here was an obstacle that had never occurred to me, for in the depths of my soul I had long regarded myself as an adult. Seeing how disconcerted I looked, the man took a sheet of paper, scribbled an address on it, and said in farewell, "Go along to the Young Communists."

The Young Communists' headquarters was in another part of the town, in a sort of caretaker's lodge attached to a somewhat tumble-down building. The boy who received me couldn't have been more than two or three years my senior. He was wearing a velvet waist-coat with the Party badge—the hammer and sickle—pinned on it. I don't know if it was just because we were both so young, or because he happened to be more affable; anyway, I felt none of the shyness which had paralyzed me an hour before, and told him what I had come for without the slightest hesitation. He at once called me "Com-rade," addressed me as "thou," and made me sit down beside him. He listened attentively, and with obvious interest, to the story of my conversion. I was amazed to hear that he hadn't read Gorki's *Mother*, which had made such a tremendous impression on me. He asked me about my family (I was rather ashamed to own up to my middle-class origin) and what I did: he then opened a folder, and after a few minutes' thought assigned me to the André Marty cell—named, as he told me, after the famous hero of the mutiny of French sailors on the Black Sea. I felt the most profound regret that I'd never heard of him, and made up my mind to make a close study of the leading Communists of the day. Heroes of novels seemed to leave the Com-rade secretary relatively cold.

He told me to come on the following Saturday (that day was, I think, Monday or Tuesday) to a meeting of the André Marty cell. There I should be given the card and badge of the Young Com-munists and start right away on my apprenticeship as a militant Communist. The "Comrade" told me, in fact, to my great delight, that the Party and its youth organizations had no use for any mere hangers-on within their ranks; the "elect" were all in duty bound to start working for the Cause without a moment's delay. As I left him with a "So long, Comrade," I felt a pride and joy such as I'd never known. True, all I'd done was to fill in a form for admission to the Young Communists, but it somehow gave me a sense of having ac-complished a great act—taken the most decisive step of my life. I felt I had "liquidated" the state of isolation which had been mine from childhood: that I was now caught up in the great sweep of history. I was sure that the passers-by must all know that I was a Communist, out to destroy all that they held dear. And yet I had no inkling of quite how far the pledge I had just made would take me

THE ANDRÉ MARTY CELL

On Saturday evening I turned up at the meeting-place of the André Marty cell three-quarters of an hour too early I strolled impatiently about the narrow streets, and on the stroke of seven went into the building, once a shop, which was now the headquarters of the cell—*my* cell.

A long plank on trestles served as a table and took up all the middle of the room. On each side of it was a long bench and, at the end, an old chair for the president. The whitewashed walls were hung with portraits of Communist leaders, and a large red flag. The president, who said his name was Louis, had been told I was coming. He made room for me near himself and gave me the badge of the Young Communists. He then called over to him the girl who acted as treasurer; I handed her my subscription, and she gave me a card which certified that I now belonged to the army of world revolution. This, at least, is how I understood the surprisingly simple little ceremony.

The room gradually filled up with girls and boys. There were about fifteen of them, the boys slightly outnumbering the girls. Although I didn't feel in the least shy, I don't remember noticing anyone in particular except the president and the girl treasurer, who had made an impression on me because she was so pretty. I was too full of anxious interest in what was going to happen to have the time, or even the wish, to notice my new companions.

That evening, for the first time in my life, I bitterly regretted not being able to sing. At a signal from the president, there was first complete silence, and then the whole gathering stood up and sang the "Internationale" and, after it, the "Young Guard." There was joy and enthusiasm in the singing, but what struck me most was the seriousness and resolution in the whole bearing of all those young people.

Although I could not join in the singing, my whole being throbbed to the rhythm of the songs. Even many years later, when I had quite lost my faith in Communism, I could never hear the "Internationale" without feeling once again the same overwhelming emotion which had swept over me on my first day as a Communist. The song, as it lived in my memory, seemed so eloquent of the hopes and sufferings of millions of men and women.

Yet it was something of a disappointment to find that the object of the meeting was not the (to me) absorbing question of revolution and the overthrow of capitalism. This meeting, in fact, was my first introduction to the humble realities of everyday life. Up to that time I had scorned any conversation that was not about books, art, or ideas, and turned up my nose at people—especially if they happened to belong to my own family—who talked about money, food or work. Now, the André Marty cell, as I learnt on that very first evening, was far more concerned with finding out all about these small, humdrum realities than with discussing great ideas. After all, weren't we professed materialists? Anyway, I was so overjoyed at belonging to a Communist cell at all that none of the matters discussed there could possibly seem commonplace, or even dull. I agreed in advance to anything they might do, anything they might ask of me.

We were only a few weeks off the seventh anniversary of the October Revolution. This was to be made the occasion for a great demonstration of the solidarity of the proletariat all over the world with the first Communist State ever to be set up. The district organizers had sent our cell a large quantity of pamphlets for distribution, and several dozen huge posters to be stuck, surreptitiously, on walls. I was new to it all; the comrades knew that I was still at school. But it never occurred to them to treat me differently from anyone else, and this filled me with affection and gratitude. I felt it showed that I was a "real" Communist; and nothing could have given me greater pleasure.

So I, too, was given a hundred pamphlets to distribute throughout the school. Just as I was leaving, Comrade Louis took me aside and advised me not to give them out openly—I didn't want to be ex-

pelled—but to slip them into my schoolfellows' pockets and satchels
without anyone's seeing. It was, no doubt, to spare my feelings as a
beginner that I was given this advice in private; in the months and
years that followed I often had reason to admire the innate delicacy
of feeling shown by boys and girls of the working class.

On Monday morning I began consciously to carry out Louis'
instructions, and very proud I felt when I saw the astonishment of
every boy in the top classes at discovering in his coat pocket a call to
join the demonstration against imperialist war, proclaim friendship
with the Soviet Union, demand wage increases, and so on. There was
even a passage about Fascism, which had just come into power in
Italy. Never in all their lives had these chips of honest, middle-class
blocks been confronted with so many things beyond their narrow
horizon—their work, flirtations, worries over pocket money, and in
the case of the best of them, their dreams of the future. Several of
them knew of my new-found enthusiasm for the founders of the revolution, but none of them guessed that it was I behind this distribution of pamphlets. I had the reputation of living in a world of books
and ideas; they would never have thought me capable of turning from
these to daring and cunning action. They did not know the marvellous
power that faith has to transform a man.

At the beginning of the week following my first cell meeting, I
proudly started wearing my badge in school—the badge which sym-
bolized the eternal alliance of peasant and worker to build a new
world. A young literature teacher, who liked me and who also was
said to be a socialist, called me into her room during the first break
and urged me not to wear the badge in school; she would, she said,
be very sorry if I were to be expelled for so trivial a matter. She had
guessed that it was I who had "planted" the pamphlets, and pointed
out that if I openly proclaimed myself a Communist it would soon
be impossible for me to do my work as a militant. I took her friendly
advice, though it went very much against the grain. But I used to take
off my badge every morning on the very doorstep of the school,
under the scornful or inquisitive eyes of the other boys; and every

evening before I went home I pinned it on again with an equal contempt for caution.

My family lived in the country, not quite twenty miles from B , and I was boarded out with friends. So it wasn't until the Christmas holidays that I could flaunt the hammer-and-sickle in my buttonhole in front of my brother and numerous cousins of both sexes—to say nothing of the grown-ups. We were at lunch, eating our *hors d'oeuvres,* when my brother, who was three years younger than I, but who loved a row and detested all my goings-on, stole up to me and tore off my badge. I protested indignantly, but it was no good; everyone backed him up, and I only just managed to dodge a cuff from my uncle. I decided to get back at them by announcing that they would see no more of me until the summer holidays. No one, not even myself, took this threat very seriously, but in fact I was never to return to the house where I had spent part of my adolescence.

THE BREATHLESS LIFE OF A MILITANT

On the Saturdays which followed this incident, I used to rejoin the comrades of my cell with all the joy one feels at meeting lifelong friends. I soon felt, indeed, as if I had known them for years—far better than I knew the boys at school, whom I met every day. It took me some time to learn the names of all my comrades of the cell, and I never found out much about them nor how they lived. But what did this objective knowledge matter? Were we not all inspired by the same faith, aflame with the same hope? From the day I joined the Young Communists, this bond meant incomparably more to me than any mere ties of blood—and on this point my views have not changed. The fact that I was called "thou" by my family and at school meant nothing to me, whereas I took it as the most gratifying compliment to be addressed as "thou" by the comrades in my cell, and by the other Communists I met during the next few years.

From March onwards, we set to work to prepare for the Labour Day demonstrations of May the First. At one of the meetings I was chosen to stick up the posters—a far more tricky job than smuggling pamphlets into the school. At 1 A.M. I met Comrade Louis. He held the glue, I carried the posters, and Comrade Anne kept watch a little way off, to warn us if a policeman came in sight. Whenever one did, we snatched up our posters, brushes and glue pots and took to our heels. Then, in some other street, we set to work anew.

The girls did not, as a rule, take part in these nocturnal expeditions. Their families would not have liked it. There were, however, exceptions, of whom Anne was an outstanding example. She was a tall, fair girl who had broken with her clergyman father and now worked as a typist and lived on her own in a servant's room. Small parties of us used to meet there to hold discussions and even, sometimes, just have fun Anne, it is true, did not really approve of fun, and here I was more on her side than were most of the others. Her abrupt, jerky manners and harsh voice might have made her unattractive, but her fearlessness in the cause of the revolution, and her extraordinary courage, compelled our admiration, and at heart we were really very fond of her. She always volunteered for the most difficult jobs and could be sent back into action day and night. All the months when I was learning how to be a militant Communist, she and I used to carry out various exploits together. Between us, we invented a very effective way of selling Communist newspapers on Sunday. We used to stand at the doors of Catholic and Protestant churches in rich neighbourhoods and shout the names of the papers at the top of our voices, always prefacing them with some religious adjective: "Buy the Christian *Vanguard!* Read the Methodist Hope!" These tactics promoted sales, but there was an awkward side to them. We had to find a new pitch every Sunday, for there was little hope of the trick's succeeding twice, and we did not want to risk a row with the beadle. Anyway, the heads of the cell decided that our method of selling newspapers did not make a sufficient contribution to "propaganda agitation," and we had to give it up.

THE FIRST OF MAY

I had given proof of considerable zeal over the spadework for the First of May demonstrations. All my spare time—which I often added to by playing truant from school—was given up to distributing pamphlets, sticking posters and selling newspapers. For two months I had not even had a moment to spare for my beloved pastime of daydreaming. The cell therefore decided that I had done the Cause good service and, with the approval of the district organizers, suggested that I should address the Youth Meeting on Labour Day. It is more than likely that the distaste for public speaking felt by most of the Young Communists had something to do with my being singled out by the district committee, and I was put down to speak for seven minutes ("neither more nor less") on the part played by the young in the struggle for peace.

It was not, I may add, the first time I had spoken in public. In the previous school year, when I wasn't quite fifteen, my gift of gab had been noticed by the principal, and I was chosen to make a speech at some function on the dangers of drink and tobacco. I didn't do badly, and ever since then, whenever a delegate had to be chosen to convey the boys' good wishes for the birthday or anniversary of the principal or one of the masters, my schoolfellows nearly always picked on me. So I didn't anticipate that I should have stage fright. This time, though, I wasn't just going to speak in front of my class, but to several hundred Young Communists, which I felt was a far weightier responsibility.

I got up my text as well as I could, cramming into it as many purple passages as possible—most of them from Barbusse's book *Le Feu*—and learnt it by heart. I then had a dress rehearsal with Comrade Louis, the head of my cell. He made me sacrifice several sentences which I had thought particularly beautiful, but which he said would mean nothing at all to young workers. For it wasn't now, as it had been at school, just a matter of rhetoric, but of convincing others, and thus of making myself understood.

On the morning of May the First I, in my role of orator, marched just behind the unfurled banner of the Young Communists, carried by the district president. As there was little fear that my voice would strike a discordant note in the singing of thousands of powerful working-class throats, I let myself go and sang at the full pitch of my lungs.

Through the words of the "Internationale" and the other revolutionary songs, I flung in the teeth of the universe my ecstatic joy and boundless faith in the victory of Communism—*our* victory. That day I felt for the first time the force of that mysterious current which flows from any mass demonstration and which, later on, often gave me the strength I needed to overcome my doubts and hesitations.

The Youth Rally took place at about noon, after the great march-past, in a square large enough to hold two or three hundred boys and girls. We had been marching for several hours with Party members, trade unionists and various other Communist or fellow-traveller organizations; we had listened to a good many speeches from our leaders, and we were all fairly tired. This, no doubt, was why it had been decided that all the speeches together were not to last more than three-quarters of an hour.

The first speaker was the "political adviser" for our district—a huge metal-worker chap; then came the "prop-agit": then I myself was hoisted onto the upturned barrel that served as a platform. My voice shook with feeling as it pronounced the sacred word "Comrades!" but it soon recovered its firmness. I felt wonderfully at my ease as I stood there in front of that crowd of young people, all of them resolved to build a new world incomparably finer than the world we knew. I was pleased, too, to see in the crowd about a dozen boys from my school, most of them members of the Poets' Club of which I was one of the founders. The loud clapping, the repeated shouts of "Down with imperialist war!" and the way the organizers of the meeting all shook hands with me, made me feel that I hadn't let the Party down too badly. In fact, I began to feel that I had now become a "notorious" Communist.

But the day after this uplifting experience, I was to see that my youthful fame had a less pleasant side to it.

A DECISIVE CHOICE

The newspapers of May 2nd of course contained accounts of the meetings and demonstrations of the previous day. The Communist papers merely gave my name in the list of speakers. The right-wing paper, on the other hand, wrote with considerable irony of the long-haired young bourgeois who had spoken with such strange venom of the social order from which his papa must draw solid profits. The writer expressed his amazement at the headmaster's allowing such pranks, and advised "Papa" to give the budding revolutionary a good hiding.

After such an article in the "decent" paper, I knew my uncle well enough to expect a visit from him that same evening. He arrived, shaking with anger, and bombarded me with reproaches: I was a disgrace to an honourable family, I had imperilled my future career as a naval officer, I was preventing my brother from starting on his. . . . When he had come to the end of all his arguments and was stung to further irritation by the impressive calm with which I took his abuse, he cried, "Either you promise here and now to get out of this pack of fanatics right away, or you never get another penny out of me."

I knew very well that the pennies in question did not come from my uncle's pocket, but had been left me by my father. I knew, too, that my uncle was only trying to frighten me. But he and I were made of the same stuff, each as proud as the other. So without a word or a moment's hesitation I took my macintosh and school bag and walked out of the house.

For a long time I roamed the streets, and then spent my first night of freedom in a public park. The ground was drenched with dew; I stretched out on a bench and tried to get a little sleep, but my imagination gave me no peace. At one moment I felt proud and glad that I was no longer a *fils de famille* but as poor as a real member of the proletariat. The next moment I thought with horror of what the unknown future might have in store. But not for one second, either that night or later, right up to this present moment, did I regret my decision or feel any wish to return to the fold.

In the morning, shivering with cold, I washed my face at the fountain and went to school as if nothing had happened. But towards the end of the day my hunger became almost unbearable, and

I found it hard to follow the lessons. I had had nothing to eat but a roll which I bought with the last pennies of my pocket money; and there had never yet been any need for me to train my stomach to go without a meal. The walk through the streets at dusk was not nearly as attractive as it had been the evening before, especially as it was beginning to drizzle and there could be no question of my sleeping in the park. I had to take refuge in a station waiting room.

On my way to school the next morning I saw a large hunk of bread in a rubbish bin. I made sure no one was looking, and pounced on it; it was hard and stale, but to me it tasted far better than the most delicious dish I'd ever eaten. During the months that followed I used often to throw a searching glance at the dust bins, and on many occasions what I found there was my one meal of the day.

Mlle P., the literature teacher who liked me, was the first person to notice that something unusual was going on. She made me tell her what had happened and tried to persuade me to change my mind about breaking with my family; when she found she couldn't, she offered to help me. She invited me to go back with her to where she lived, and gave me something to eat; for several nights after that, I slept on the carpet in her room. This could not, of course, go on indefinitely, for I knew I was putting her to expense. I thought out all sorts of plans for earning my living, but I was too entirely inexperienced to be able, unaided, to find the best practical way of setting about it. Mlle P. wasn't much better in such matters than I myself. I had to put my pride in my pocket, tell the head of my cell, Comrade Louis, what had happened and ask his advice.

He was obviously astounded at my having broken with my family. He himself was the son of working-class parents and it had seemed to him only logical to join the Young Communists as soon as he realized his status in the world. He had never given a thought to the problems that might arise when boys of the middle classes took the same step.

He didn't try to hide the fact that I was too young to find work in a factory or an office. Nor could there be any question of my becoming an apprentice somewhere, for the simple reason that I shouldn't earn enough to live on. He, like Mlle P., advised me to carry on with my work at school, for the proletariat "needed militants with a good solid intellectual equipment." As regarded the main problem, we should just have to wait for circumstances to give us a lead.

THE SOLIDARITY OF THE WORKING CLASSES

The very next day, Louis told me that I could sleep at the cell headquarters up to the end of the school year. He and some of the other comrades had put their heads together to get me what I needed, one of them producing an old mattress, another a pillow, another a blanket. With a tact and naturalness that one might well seek in vain in any other class, these young working boys and girls somehow managed to bring me a hot and fairly decent meal every evening. On Saturdays, when they'd got their pay, they always gave up some of their meagre pocket money so that I shouldn't be quite penniless. I was not yet used to the wonderful simplicity of the working class and felt terribly ashamed of living on their charity. But I had no alternative; and this state of affairs went on for over two months.

At the end of the school year it became quite impossible for me to stay any longer at B., where at any moment I might run into one of my family. I was particularly afraid of my mother's using emotional blackmail to induce me to go home. So, on the advice of Louis and Mlle P., I decided to move to another town and even another part of the country. Without quite knowing why, I set out for N., an important university and industrial town, where I knew that the Communist Party was strongly entrenched.

As I came warmly recommended by the district organizer of the Young Communists at B., the Communists of N. received me with open arms. One of them, who worked in an office, invited me to share his room; another got his parents to give me a camp bed; others did all they could to settle me as comfortably as possible. Once again I saw with my own eyes that a situation which would have been hopeless, or at least extremely difficult, among well-to-do young people of the middle class was simplicity itself among these young workers who had nothing.

As I had to earn a living, it was decided that I should sell Communist books from door to door. Every morning, therefore, I filled a small suitcase with Soviet novels and Party booklets on topics of the day, and set off on my round of ringing door bells. In the prosperous parts of the town I didn't do much business. At working-class homes, on the other hand, I seldom failed to sell something, especially at the beginning of the month. It didn't bring me in much, but it was enough to buy bread, a little meat, and sometimes fruit. Two or three times during the three months when I was carrying on this trade, I even managed to get myself a hot meal in a working-class restaurant. The reader need not pity me; one never really appreciates food at its full value until one feels a great craving for it. And I have always preferred a short moment of intense happiness to the colourless pleasures of habit.

I couldn't go on being a travelling bookseller for very long. I should soon have made the round of all the houses whose owners might buy books or pamphlets from me, and I couldn't keep turning up too often to the same people. Above all, I still had a year of secondary school ahead of me, and I had to find some kind of work that would fit in with the hours of the classes.

During my last two months at B. I had written various articles for the local Communist newspaper describing working-class demonstrations; and my comrades had thought them pretty good. So I decided to offer my services to the editor of the Communist daily at N., and was taken on as a copy writer to record local events. Every evening after school (and this went on for a year) I used to go round to the police station for information about the crimes and accidents which had taken place since the previous day. If there had been anything really outstanding, I always tried to see the inspector in charge of the case, in the hopes of getting a few additional details out of him. Sometimes, too, I went to the scene of the crime or accident to give my readers the touches of local colour they liked I used to spend almost the whole of every Thursday at the law courts. Almost every week, too, I had to take off two or three days from school to attend trials which the editor thought interesting. Then, when I'd sent in my account to the paper, I used to go along to the meetings of the cell or district, for since April 1925 I'd been head of propaganda ("agit-prop" in the Communist jargon) among the Young Communists of N. I didn't, as a rule, get back till late at night, and then I had to set to again on my homework.

At sixteen one isn't really a very accomplished journalist, and it was my solidarity with the Party rather than any professional merits that had induced the editor to take me on. I earned very little—just enough to keep from starving. I gradually became used to having a proper meal only every other day, and barely felt it as a hardship; on off-days I made do with a piece of bread. There could, of course, be no question of my buying new clothes; I still wore the shirt and pants which I had on when I first broke with my family. At B., Comrade Anne, the clergyman's daughter, had made me give her my underclothes every week so that she could wash them, and I always spent half the day without them, waiting for them to dry. At N., the comrade who let me share his room had my underclothes washed with his. For some time I managed to hide from him the fact that I had nothing to change to, but one day he found out. He said nothing to me, but suggested to the other members of the cell that they should club together and buy me a shirt, a pair of pants and some socks. Later on, when I simply had to have another suit and some more socks, I again turned travelling bookseller during the school holidays, and went about over all the villages and small towns in the neighbourhood. My life was certainly far harder than the lives of even the poorest of my companions, but I had the glorious feeling that it was for a great cause; far from being depressing, it was profoundly satisfying.

The only family I had now was the family of young Communists, but it was enormous, with ramifications all over the world. The cell I joined when I arrived at N. was an important one, with twenty members. Two of them were typists from the lower middle class; all the others were working-class men and girls. Unless one has belonged to a cell of Young Communists, it is hard to have any idea of the intensity with which the ideal of comradeship is translated into action. I know very well—it is a point I shall come back to—that Christian charity is infinitely more beautiful and above all incomparably wider in its range than Communist solidarity, which is rigidly restricted to those fighting for the same cause. Even so, when I became a Christian and started involuntarily comparing either my seminary or the religious communities I had seen from the inside with the Young Communist cell, almost always, as far as concrete realities were concerned, the comparison went in favour of the cell. It had altogether more simplicity, more spontaneity.

It takes a newcomer some little time to get used to the "naturalness" of working-class solidarity. It was months—years, even—before I learnt to accept the help given me with the simplicity of those who offered it. I remember, for instance, a week-end camp in a forest, on a bank of a great river. A score or so of boys and girls were at this camp, and someone—who, I don't know—let out the story of my break with my family and the difficult time I was having. One of my comrades started a collection to help me. She was—unfortunately in the circumstances—a very lovely girl, and when she came over to give me the proceeds of the collection, all the prejudices of my middle-class upbringing rose within me. I felt insulted and humiliated, refused the money, and fled into the wood. But I had seen from the look on my comrades' faces how mistaken and incomprehensible my attitude seemed to them. They had been glad to give up whatever they could—the money which would have bought a packet of cigarettes, perhaps, or a lipstick—to help a friend in need, and regarded it as a matter of course that he would accept it in the same simple spirit. The district leader, who was older than the others and better acquainted with the stupid prejudices of the middle class, had to explain to them why I behaved as I did. He took the money and came to give it to me himself. He showed me how silly I had been to refuse the help of my *comrades* and made me heartily ashamed of myself for having behaved "like a dirty little bourgeois."

The reason I had done so was the thought of how my cousins and their friends would have treated anyone who infringed the conventions of their set, and I dreaded the jibes and contempt of my companions. The comrade who brought me the money persuaded me to go back to the camp, where I found that everyone seemed to have forgotten the incident. The money itself was welcome enough (my shoes had no soles to them), but what brought the tears to my eyes in a wave of emotional gratitude was the wonderful, instinctive delicacy of feeling which now seems only to exist among working people —especially the thinking section of the working people.

THE DIFFICULTIES OF ASSIMILATION

As time went on I couldn't help seeing that there was, after all, a barrier between me and the others in the cell. They were as conscious of it as I was. I was poorer than any of them; I had no family—no home, even. They showed me unfailing friendliness; they would have done anything to help me. They even had a certain admiration for me because of my fanatical work for the Party. Whatever it was— sticking posters, distributing pamphlets, selling newspapers or going off to give elementary Marxist teaching to new cells just starting on the outskirts of the town or in the neighbouring villages—they all knew I was ready to do whatever was asked of me, and usually more. And that counts with Young Communists.

Yet they knew instinctively that I was not like themselves. It wasn't just because I'd gone to a lycée instead of becoming apprenticed. There were quite a number of lycée pupils in the various Young Communist cells in the town, and as a rule there was no dividing line between them and their working-class comrades. This was because the lycée pupils also came from families which, if not working-class, were at least drawn from the lower class. Their parents lived more or less like the parents of their companions; they themselves had gone to the same primary schools as the future apprentices; it was natural that they should talk the same language and be interested in the same problems of everyday life as the young workers.

For all my extreme, sub-proletarian, poverty, I was looked on as an "aristocrat," and "intellectual." I had had no hesitations and no regrets over giving up my family and an extremely pampered life But it was a very different matter when it came to giving up a certain bohemian style of living. I still went about with long hair and loud ties. I was undoubtedly quite as sincere a Communist as the others, but I was a very ostentatious one. It was not until much later that I saw what an embarrassment my behaviour must have been to my comrades, whose Communism came to them as naturally as Catholicism to a Breton.

At the meetings there was no visible distinction between them and myself. I probably irritated them at times by my taste for rhetoric and my over-ebullient enthusiasm, but no one ever said so, and I myself never noticed it. It wasn't until the meetings were over and private life began that one saw the difference. I had no home and no family, and consequently no private life. I had thought at first that this was true of all "real" Communists: I imagined their whole lives spent in ceaseless expectation of the revolution. I soon saw that this was not so at all—that once they left the cell behind them, my comrades were swallowed up in the crowd of their own district or factory.

They almost always left the meetings in small bands of boys and girls. Naturally enough, I used to fall in with one or other of these groups—whichever I happened to come across. But I couldn't help noticing, bad psychologist though I was, that my presence always produced a certain embarrassment—or at any rate, that it obviously wasn't wanted. Apart from outings and camps officially organized by the Young Communists, I was never invited to take part in any of their social activities—their excursions or Sunday night hops. I was small, too thin, and badly dressed; I looked "less of a man" than other boys of my age. But this wasn't what mattered. What mattered was that I was not like the others. Even in the streets or on any outing, the only thing I wanted to talk about was Communism—or else some book which no one else had read. The others, too, were Communists to the marrow of their bones, but they took an interest in football and basketball matches, played pelota, and enjoyed discussing their work and the things and people of their neighbourhood. They entered into the amusements of other young people of their class and sang, not only revolutionary songs, but the hit tunes of the day. It was in all these ways that I was so unlike them. With the best will in the world, I could not take the least interest in such "futilities."

One Saturday evening I overheard some of my companions arranging to meet on Sunday evening for a dance, at an eating place whose address I knew. As I had just bought a new suit and had my shoes resoled, I very much wanted to go with them. My solitude sometimes got on my nerves, and moreover I was beginning to be interested in girls. I was very proud of my singularity, but more and more often I felt a longing to bring my life into step with the lives of other people.

The dance took place in a kind of shed attached to the eating-house. All along the walls there were small tables on trestles; the middle of the room was the dance floor. The "orchestra" consisted of a violin and two accordions. Although I was not at all shy, I had to overcome a strange feeling of awkwardness before I could bring myself to enter this haunt of cheap pleasure—a feeling I should certainly not have had in a more "select" environment.

When I went in, I saw at once, sitting in a corner, Charles, Lucienne and Annie, all three members of my cell, with two other young people whom I didn't know. They were clearly astonished to see me, but they made room for me in a friendly way near Annie, and Charles stood me to a glass of red wine. I did my best to join in their conversation, but it wasn't any good. When, for instance, I tried to tell them what I'd been reading in the last number of *Friends of the U.S.S.R.*, or give them my views on the revolutionary movements springing up all over the world, they pretended not to hear and went on gossiping about things which seemed to me to have no interest at all. Yet I knew these three members of my cell very well—quite well enough to know that they were none of them tongue-tied about their convictions. I had too little experience of life to know that there is a time for everything, and that a local dance is hardly the setting for a discussion of books and revolutions. Workingmen, quite as much as the middle classes—even more than they, in fact—have their own social code.

The boys sat making what I thought coarse comments on the girls as they danced; the girls laughed in what seemed to me a most undignified way. I found it hard to believe that these were the same people who only the day before had been studying the principles of Marxist-Leninism with such passionate interest—people with whom I had often had difficult jobs to do for the Party. When I saw Charles drinking too much red wine, roaring out in a way that shocked my still deeply rooted puritanism, I felt his behaviour unworthy of a Communist. Lucienne herself apparently saw nothing out of the way in his overfamiliarity, and made no attempt to ward off his—as I thought—disrespectful hands. Later on, I came very slowly to see that the only Communists who make a point of trying to live like ascetics are those of middle-class origin, to whom the mere fact of being a Communist invests anyone with a halo of heroism and romance.

As everyone was dancing, I felt I ought to dance too. I asked Annie to be my partner, as she was the only girl in our group who hadn't a man with her that evening. In contrast to middle-class convention, it was unusual in that community for a boy to ask a girl to dance with him if she had come with some other boy—unless, of course, there was an exchange of "good turns" between friends. Annie looked astonished at my invitation, but she accepted it. I had been taught to dance by my cousins, but I found it quite impossible to keep in time with the frenzied rhythm of this working-class ball. I kept tripping up, treading on my partner's feet, bumping into other couples, apologizing. . . . The unfortunate girl was clearly undergoing agonies at being made to look so ridiculous; she must have known how much she would be teased about it next day at the workshop. My long hair, my flaming red tie, my too-small, too-white hands, were making everyone stare at us. At that time I hardly realized how much members of the working class dislike being made conspicuous. Well, it was my first dance of that kind, and the last. Later on, when I was higher up in the Party, I had sometimes to attend meetings where there was dancing, but I always had the sense to stay in my corner and not expose any more girls to humiliation.

IMMORALITY OR THE NEW MORALITY?

I also found out gradually that almost all the boys and girls of the Communist Youth cell were paired off into lovers. Not that the word "lover" existed in their vocabulary. A girl was said to have a lover only if she was known to be the mistress of a "bourgeois," especially if he were her employer. The words "lover" and "mistress," as my comrades used them, always had a pejorative meaning. It was under the title of "my friend" that one introduced the boy or girl to whom one had given one's heart.

The so-called immorality of Communists comes in for a good deal of unfavourable comment among Christians. It is true, of course, that Communists do not conform to the principles and laws of Christian morality. But as they are not Christians, can one logically hold this against them? As for ordinary middle-class morality, not as it is supposed to be but as it really is, it seems to me to owe little more to the spirit of the Gospels than does Communist morality, and to have a strong dash of lies and hypocrisy into the bargain.

When two comrades entered into very intimate relations, they did not, of course, go about advertising the fact, but they did not hide it either. Other Communists regarded it as perfectly right and proper that the two "friends" should sell newspapers and distribute pamphlets together. In the same way, no one at a camp thought it strange if some couple slipped off to spend the night in a lonely barn—though, in the communal tent, everyone had to be on his best behaviour. At work-meetings, on the other hand, any sign of affection or even of preference was frowned on. Most important of all, love must never be allowed to hinder the work of a militant Communist. When I had become a Christian, I was amazed to find that even priests almost always think it quite right and proper for young Christians to stop all their apostolic activities the moment they become engaged. Communist ethics would never tolerate such a desertion.

Even today, in middle-class society and among those who have accepted its principles, the virginity of young girls wears an almost mystical halo, and its loss is hushed up like some appalling calamity. To my comrades, on the other hand, virginity seemed to have no prestige at all. No one was in the least surprised if a girl of sixteen (or sometimes less) had a "friend"; even her parents took it without a murmur. This "sexual freedom" was, however, balanced by the duty, almost always insisted on, of unswerving fidelity. What, in "good society," is known as flirting was extremely rare, and always strongly condemned. As soon as it became known that some girl was the "friend" of a comrade, *morality* forbade anyone to pay her attentions, just as it would not allow any man who had a "friend" to make up to another woman.

The symptoms of pregnancy were usually taken as a signal that the time had come to get married at the Town Hall. But fairly often, especially during the troubled '30's, marriage was ruled out, or made extremely difficult, by unemployment or the impossibility of finding anywhere to live. In such cases one came to accept without surprise the fact that some couple, who were not married and not even living together, should have children. If, on the other hand, the man abandoned the woman and child, he was severely censured and almost always made to leave the Party. A certain prominent Communist had seized his opportunity, when a comrade was imprisoned for his activities during a strike, to set up house with the other man's "friend." He incurred the usual penalty, and even had his parliamentary mandate withdrawn.

It must not, however, be assumed from what I have said that exemplary virtue flourishes among all Communists, or even among the most fervent. There were cases of divorce and remarriage among them. It also happened from time to time that "friends" who were not married, parted, because one of them had fallen in love with someone else. Communist "morality" took this in its stride. The one thing it did insist on was that it should be done "decently," without harming the Party. Every self-respecting Communist had a moral duty, if he wanted to change his "friend," to tell her so frankly; the same held good for women, if the initiative came from their side. The Party knew from experience that openly admitted love affairs almost never hindered the work of militants, whereas little hole-and-corner carryings-on nearly always led to disaster. The secretary of a certain district leader had for years been the wife of a Communist deputy. Then she left him, and became the "friend" of another leading Communist. Everyone would have thought it scandalous and nonsensical if the situation had disrupted the collaboration and good relations of the two men; and the woman went on working in various organizations with her ex-husband. Jealousy, in fact, was regarded as a shameful middle-class complex, part of that "category of having" (to use a term dear to Gabriel Marcel) which every Communist should repudiate as heresy. This does not mean, of course, that every Communist goes through life without a twinge of jealousy. I myself came across several dramas of which jealousy was the sole cause—cases of women who were deserted and committed suicide, and, still more often, of fervent militants who refused to accept the situation when the. ·ives or "friends" transferred their affections to some other comrade—especially if he stood higher in the Communist hierarchy—and broke openly and violently with the Party.

On the whole, my girl comrades liked me. They seemed quite pleased to do me small services such as mending my underclothes and darning my socks. They were sorry for me because I was so helpless in practical matters. They were often more sensitive and perceptive than the boys of their class; my type of eloquence, less rough-and-ready than that of the working-class militants, appealed to them; and they liked my books and articles. But if I had taken this to mean that any of them had any special feeling for me, or would agree to becoming my "friend," I should very soon have found out my mistake. The inborn common sense of the working people warned them not to look for a deep or lasting relationship with any comrade who came, as I did, from the middle class. They knew instinctively that we were too unlike them in our tastes and interests for our love to be anything but a passing infatuation. Certain young men of the middle class, who had heard of the advanced sexual freedom of the Communist youth clubs, used to attend them in the hope of picking up girls. Unless they were carried away by the atmosphere and became genuine militant Communists, they soon cleared out, disappointed men.

What I have just said does not, of course, apply to the lower middle and working class as a whole. We all know that many little typists and shopgirls dream of nothing better than having a "real gentleman" as a "friend." But militant Communists, who regard themselves as the incarnation of the true proletarian spirit, bear roughly the same relation to most of the working class as the best Jécists and Jocists, or Boy Scout patrol leaders, bear to most young Christians whose Christianity never goes beyond the observances of a few traditional rites.

YOUNG MIDDLE-CLASS COMMUNISTS

In almost every Communist cell, at N. as elsewhere, there were some boys and girls who could not claim to be victims of capitalist exploitation. These were the sons and daughters of industrialists, rich tradespeople, or even noble families whose names are familiar to everyone who knows the history of France. These young students (for, with very few exceptions, all the young middle-class Communists were students) would be told, following the fluctuations of Party opportunism, now to join the cell of their district, so as to mingle on friendly terms with working-class militants; now to form cells composed entirely of students, on the pattern of the cells organized for the workers. In these student cells we certainly felt very much more at our ease than among working-class companions. But the segregation carried serious dangers with it.

We young students, with no experience whatever of practical life, and an exaggerated liking for theoretical discussion, often failed to see the importance of some humdrum militant task. Though we hadn't much discernment, we were able to give a passable imitation of the manners and customs of our working-class comrades. These, however, unfortunately bore no relation to our own instincts and spontaneous reactions, and the result was nearly always disastrous. Whether we liked it or not, we were in fact the offshoots of a decadent social class, in which lies and hypocrisy have taken the place of the frankness and simplicity that are the general rule among the poor. And so sexual freedom, which seldom led to trouble among our working-class comrades, in our case turned all too easily to mere loose living. We didn't hide our love affairs any more than the workers did, but the objects of them were always changing.

One must remember that to most of these young middle-class Communists, especially the girls, membership of the Party did not imply any very definite commitment. Quite a number joined it out of snobbery, or because they were on the lookout—unconsciously, it is true —for some kind of nervous titillation—just as some people go to surrealist clubs or haunt the centres of existentialism. Quite often the girls were Communists only because they were in love with Communist boys who had persuaded them into it. Most of them tired of it pretty quickly and went back to their own set, when of course they had once more to conform to its moral code. This inevitably led to a certain lack of wholeheartedness in their attitude, both to Communism and to their original background.

In my opinion, there is no reason to doubt the sincerity of most young Communists of middle-class origin. At the beginning, their motive, like mine, was usually a sense of revolt against their family and background; at that stage, their Communism was mainly negative. But there were a great many who, after a time, played quite a sincere and devoted part in the struggle to bring about a better world. They were quite willing to learn from books, or, still more effectively, from the example of their working-class comrades. I knew only very few who refused to accept any work that was ordered or suggested by the Party. In fact, they were often keener and more noisily enthusiastic than the workers, who often accused them of a certain infantilism—unjustly, for the real trouble was a lack of balance inevitable in people straddled midway between a middle-class past and a Communist present. As I have said, we were the only ones to practise a certain "revolutionary asceticism." To serve the Cause more effectively, many of us gave up tobacco and alcohol; some even thought it their duty to maintain almost complete chastity. This had nothing to do with any law or principle of morality, either religious or natural; it was inspired solely by the thought of what would best promote revolutionary efficiency—just as athletes before some contest go into strict training so as to be at the top of their form.

As we strolled in small groups through the broad streets and avenues of the prosperous part of the town (where some of us lived), we used to enjoy discussing the revolution that lay ahead. It was delightful to think of all the upheavals it would cause in these very streets. We would plan how some ornate church would be turned into a dance hall for the people; how the Protestant church would become a day nursery; we imagined factory workers and even rag-and-bone men living in the beautiful houses. If by any chance some working-class boy was in our little party and heard our wonderful dreams for the future, he would not only refuse to share them, but usually took us to task with considerable force for being so childish. The workers were more realistic than we, and more mature; they seemed to know by instinct that after the revolution, as before, factory workers would not live in fine houses. Those would all be taken over by the commissars.

We used, too, to amuse ourselves by sharing our future commissarships among ourselves; the young workers wouldn't join in that game either. To them, Communism meant simply a form of society in which the workingman would be able to earn a decent living; in which he would be protected against insecurity, and no longer see the desperate poverty of some people insulted by the luxury of others; and in which, if he had the wish and ability, he could go on studying. This probably explains why workingmen are not in the least shocked when people hold forth to them about the privileges of the leading Communists in the Soviet Union, or the château where the head of the French Communist Party lives. I have noticed, hundreds if not thousands of times, that the ideal of equality means much less to them than to middle-class revolutionaries, who really are scandalized, as the workers are not, by the new inequalities within the Soviet Union. The workingman is a Communist because he wants to have some chance in life; the bourgeois, because he wants to realize a theory, an ideal. In one sense, and I do not mean it to be taken as at all an unfavourable one, it is true to say that the working-class revolutionary is a materialist, and the middle-class revolutionary an idealist, even and especially when he professes historical materialism.

I was one of the few students whom my working-class comrades took more or less seriously. I was not, as I have said, looked on as being quite one of them. They didn't much want to be on terms of personal friendship with me, and the girls didn't like to be seen with me in their own part of the town. The only thing that seemed to make it all right was if I was selling newspapers with them, or handing out leaflets. But everyone kept in mind that I had broken with my own family and background and was leading a very hard life. The other young middle-class Communists, who were still living with their families in fashionable parts of the town, were made use of to carry out certain kinds of work, but no one had entire confidence in them, or was particularly surprised when, after a few months—at best a few years—of Communism, they turned their backs on it and followed in Father's footsteps in business or industry or one of the professions.

It was my lot, after ten or twenty years, to meet many old friends who had once been Communists. They had now settled down, and although almost all had very happy memories of their Communist days, they spoke of them with the ironic detachment with which one refers to the follies of one's youth. Respectable mothers of families seemed to have forgotten the time when, to show their emancipation from middle-class traditions, they used without a qualm to suggest to some boy they liked that he should sleep with them. And those who had succeeded in sleeping with a Communist who really *was* a workingman were extremely proud of it.

Middle-class Communists, who made loose living the test of their break with the old world, did not seem to notice that their working-

class comrades never advocated free love and always stood up reso-
lutely for faithfulness and constancy. But, as I have said, among
middle-class Communists the destructive element was very much in
the ascendancy over the constructive. To understand why this is so,
we shall find the dialectic of Sartre more illuminating than that of
Marx. False as Sartre's explanation of existence is when applied to
most men, it is undoubtedly true of a certain degenerate section of the
middle class.

But I am anticipating. In the two years (1925–7) which I spent
as a militant in the ranks of the Young Communists, Sartre had not
yet written anything, and I myself never attempted to explain my
own or my companions' conduct by depth psychology. There were
days when I suffered somewhat on account of my loneliness. I felt it
particularly on holidays, when everyone else was at home with his
family. It seemed to me scandalous that most of the working-class
Communists, even the most "enlightened" and active, continued to
keep the Christian feast days, especially Christmas. They did not, it is
true, tell their children that Jesus had been born in Bethlehem, or
give the day any religious significance. But there were very few Communist homes without a special meal, toys for the children, and even,
in many cases, a Christmas tree. This both amazed me and increased
my feeling of isolation. But I had not reached an age when one is
really able to suffer. My studies, my work as a journalist, and all that
I had to do as a militant Communist, filled, and more than filled, my
day. I had only four or five hours out of the twenty-four left for
sleep; and this state of affairs was to last for ten years.

OUR JEWISH COMRADES

Among the young middle-class Communists, a very high proportion were of Jewish birth. I have noticed the same thing in many
European countries. I was not at that time able to bring the light of
psychology to bear on human reactions, and found it hard to understand why, even more than Christians, the sons and daughters of

Jewish capitalists were drawn to Communism. But I gradually came
to see what lay behind this phenomenon. These young Jews were,
like all of us, in a state of revolt against the narrowness and routine of
their family circle, and longed for emancipation. Added to this was
the age-old reaction of a racial minority which for thousands of
years has been despised and persecuted. I had hardly ever come across
any Jews as a boy, and was surprised to learn how greatly, even in
countries as liberal-minded as France, Great Britain, Belgium and
Switzerland, most of them suffer from a complex of being *foreigners.*
And this was particularly noticeable in those who made out that
they were completely assimilated. By joining a revolutionary party
they were acting, though perhaps unconsciously, out of inherited
hatred of a world which, rightly or wrongly, they considered hostile
to Jews.

In the Young Communist organization, our Jewish comrades
fought, vigorously and tenaciously, against the separatist tendencies
of their race. Their wish to mix with non-Jews even went too far at
times. As they were easily hurt, they were quick to accuse other people of being anti-Semitic when, in most cases, it was simply a case
of personal likes or dislikes into which racial considerations did not
enter at all. Only in one or two central European countries, notably
Poland and Rumania, anti-Semitism had invaded even the Communist Party, which had to form separate organizations for Poles, Jews
and Rumanians. But, except in these countries, it would never have
occurred to working-class militant Communists to ask the nationality
of a comrade. They found it hard to understand the Jewish girls in
our cells, who made it a point of honour, as though it were the
crowning achievement of their emancipation, to be known as the
"friend" of a non-Jewish comrade.

The slight caution which the militants often showed with regard
to Jewish comrades had nothing to do with racialism. To begin with,
most of these young Jews came from far more capitalistic back-
grounds than the other Young Communist students. Even at N.,
where there were not very many Jews, we had among us the son and
two daughters of well-known bankers, the daughter of one of the

richest siderurgists in Europe, and so on. It was hard to believe that
they had in all sincerity taken up the class struggle on the side of the
proletariat. Besides—and this was the main consideration—outside
Central Europe, where most of the Party leaders were Jews, it was,
almost everywhere, very unusual for young Jews not to return to the
capitalist fold within two or three years of finishing their studies. It
was still more unusual to find any who broke with tradition by marry-
ing non-Jews. Everyone, of course, knew this, and it explained why a
certain psychological barrier separated the Jews from the others, even
in Communist organizations. Both by their exaggerated wish, in the
early stages, to show that they were no different from anyone else,
and by the fact that they were almost certain, sooner or later, to play
the part of the Prodigal Son, it was they who set themselves apart.

THE HEAD OF "AGIT-PROP"

Hardly a year after I had joined the Young Communists, I was put
in charge of the work of propaganda and agitation for the whole
district of N. My activities now had a whole *département* to range
over. This did not mean, of course, that I gave up all active work in
my cell. Both to set a good example to the "militants at the base" and
to keep in touch with the concrete work of the Party, all Communists
of higher rank continued to belong to their respective cells. So off I
went from time to time, with other members of my cell, to hand out
pamphlets and sell newspapers. But my real work now lay elsewhere.

I had to share out, among the Young Communist cells of the
district, the propaganda material sent to us from the national centre;
to see that it was usefully distributed, and pass on local needs to the
national centre of agit-prop. I found that I had, more and more, to
travel about over the *département,* in order to give the heads of the
various cells verbal explanations of our orders for propaganda. If I'd
been a workingman, I should probably have had the burden of earning a living taken off my shoulders and been given the small but
adequate pay allotted to the permanent staff. But the heads of the

Party did not like a *ci-devant* bourgeois put on its permanent staff;
they were afraid that the Party might lose some of its purely proletarian character. So I had to go on earning my living by the journalistic odd-jobs which had been given me when I arrived at N. As before, I seldom had enough to eat; the only well-fed days were those
when I had just arrived at a new place and was asked to a meal by
the family of some local official. But these material difficulties didn't
bother me much, and I never stopped to think that things might have
been otherwise. It was not until some years later, when I was telling
other people about my life at that time, that it struck me as having
been fairly unusual.

The most surprising part of it was, I think, that I was able to
finish my secondary school. But even that caused me no surprise
until I saw how difficult many young people seem to find it to pass
their final examinations, even when they have nothing else to think
about—whereas examinations were the very last things that ever
worried me. Yet I don't think I was more brilliant than other boys,
though I was certainly not shown any favouritism. But I had a good
memory, excellent health, and I liked work. And above all I was terribly proud. I wanted at all costs to show my family that I could succeed without them. And I knew that, whatever else I might succeed
in, if I failed in examinations, they would feel they were in the right.

The problem which at that time least preoccupied or even interested me was unquestionably religion. Atheism was an understood
thing—in fact, obligatory—among Young Communists. There must
have been many, especially among the working-class members, whose
families were practising Catholics or Protestants. Almost all of them
had probably made the Solemn Communion which in France follows
First Communion. With few exceptions, they thought religion so
unimportant that they never bothered to talk about it. But for strict
Party orders, I think most of them wouldn't have minded getting
married in church, "to please the old folk." They looked on it as a
mere convention, like going to the photographer's. Some of them
were so utterly indifferent to religion that they could not understand
why the Party should attach so much importance to it, and did not

feel they were being in the least disloyal if they occasionally went to religious ceremonies.

Of all the students, the only ones who hotly denied that their ancestral faith had had any influence on their development were the Jews. Some of the others probably came from Christian families and had had a more or less specifically Christian education. I remember one girl in particular—Françoise—who joined us while she was still at a convent school. She had decided to become a Communist during a period of revolt against the Reverend Mother, who had accused her (unjustly, according to her) of bad behaviour. One Sunday she and I went off together to sell newspapers. We happened to pass a church and, out of sheer force of habit, she crossed herself. She was terribly ashamed of having done so, and at once tried to make up for it by behaving in a way startlingly at variance with what she had learnt at home and in the convent. By the end of the month, no one could count the number of lovers she had had, each for one night. Surprising as it may seem, she never left the Communist Party, and now, a quarter of a century later, she is still a militant.

Whatever our religious background, I don't remember one conversation on religion with the other comrades. In the case of some of them, there was probably a complex of human respect which kept them off a subject that was so much looked down on by the Party. But most of them simply felt, as I did, that there was no problem. We almost all belonged to the Association of Freethinkers; we listened meekly, and with unconcealed boredom, to the lectures on atheism which the heads of the Party felt it their duty to give us; but all this had no bearing on the matters which really filled our thoughts. If we ever happened to come on some religious demonstration, the most we bothered to do was to make a few coarse jokes. Those whose families still practised some form of religion had, more often than the others, to take a strong line, as by refusing to go to church for some baptism, marriage or funeral; but they didn't talk about it any more than did the rest of us. And yet we, at least, the "intellectuals," had an absolute passion for debates and discussions of all kinds. But every social group has its taboos.

If one can trust the experience of psychologists who have specialized in the study of the unconscious, it seems very likely that our wholly negative attitude to religion came from the fact that our counter-certainties were not so strongly held as we ourselves believed.

3 The Dogmas of Marxist Faith

The reader has already seen that Marxist doctrine had played no part in my conversion to Communism. It could not have been otherwise, for I knew nothing whatever about it. In the first few months after I joined the Young Communists, I was completely absorbed in the thousand-and-one duties which every militant has to carry out. I went, like all the others, to the lectures given by Party instructors on Marxist-Leninist theory, and I also read a great many booklets. But all this was very elementary. The Party asked more of its intellectuals.

As I have said, I was put in charge of the Young Communist propaganda in our district. It was then my work to instruct others. Now propaganda, as Communists understand it, has two sides to it— one exoteric, the other esoteric. The exoteric mainly consists in passing on—through pamphlets, posters, newspaper articles and discussions—whatever the current slogans may be. The important thing is to know how to adapt oneself to the minds and interests of one's audience.

The esoteric side of propaganda sets out to give militant Communists as solid a grounding in Marxism as possible; and here again the receptive capacity of each individual is taken into account.

Even when I had finished with the lycée I still went on reading philosophy; in fact, I read it with even more absorption than before, now that I was not just trying to cram in what I should need for my *baccalauréat* in the following spring. Every moment that wasn't taken up with my journalistic work or militant's duties, I spent reading philosophy. It goes without saying that the exponents of Marxism —Hegel, Marx, Engels, Lenin, Plekhanov and the rest—held pride of place. But I didn't neglect Kant, Leibniz, James, Dürkheim, Lévy-Bruhl, Brunschvicg, Bergson. To appease my Marxist conscience when it gave me twinges over the many hours I spent reading "bourgeois" philosophy, I used to tell myself that I had to know them in order to refute them Yet I had to admit to myself that the writings of some of these "heretics" gave me far more pleasure than the works recommended by the Party. Bergson, in particular, fascinated me. At that time I used often to regret that none of the exponents of Communism had such magic in the use of words; I felt sure that a Marxist counterpart of Bergson would win over a great many young intellectuals—who are nearly always more alive to the form than the content. Later on, I was to have much the same feeling as regards Christian thinkers, among whom, again, there are very few born writers. But it is not given to everyone to be an artist—and it would seem that, among philosophers, artists are even harder to come by than elsewhere.

When I had passed my *baccalauréat,* I was sent to Paris for three months to follow an advanced course in Marxism. Of our professors, some were quite good, others very poor. Some taught us the economic theories of Marxism; others, the Hegelian basis of dialectical materialism, or the application of Marxist method to science; others again, the history of the Workers' movement, and socialism. Of all the men who taught us, the one I liked best was Georges Politzer, a professor of philosophy and an excellent teacher. He had the art of presenting the driest theories of Marxism in an extremely clear way, yet without losing any of their essentials. Even workingmen without any secondary education got a great deal out of his lectures. In my own case, he taught me what for many years was to be extremely useful to me— a method indispensable to any profound study of Marxism. It was he, too, who showed me that it is possible to teach philosophy effectively even to quite uneducated people

THE THEORY OF ECONOMIC CONTRADICTIONS

The first thing every Marxist has to know is the economic contradictions of capitalist society. I therefore read, with particular care, the chapters in *Das Kapital* which deal with trade, rates of exchange, the circulation of goods, the transformation of money into capital, work, the production of surplus value, wages and the accumulation of capital. Even this list is far from being complete. I cannot honestly say that I read these chapters with any great pleasure. I had no personal experience of economic matters and found it hard to take a genuine interest in Marx's terribly abstract speculations. Quite often I failed to grasp either their meaning or their range. Anyhow, as I was soon to learn, there are few Communists, even high up in the Party, who have waded through more than the first volume of *Das Kapital;* most of them find it quite enough to read selected extracts and commentaries. I myself read, and even reread, all three volumes, but at the cost of considerable boredom. It wasn't until much later, when I had acquired a deeper knowledge of the economic sciences, that I was able to subject *Das Kapital* to critical analysis. One must, in fact, be well up in the economic theories of the eighteenth and nineteenth centuries if one is to fit Marxism into its historic context. As soon as I had this knowledge I could not fail to see that where economic science was concerned, Marx was far less original than most of his followers suppose.

But, for the time being, what most stuck in my mind was the purely human aspect of these economic Marxist theories. The oversimplification of the theory of surplus value, which made it appear self-evidently right, could not fail to take in a boy of sixteen. Was it likely that I should be able to see through the idea that work alone produces value? For (so Marxist theory assures us), even those things which seem to us most precious are quite valueless as long as they remain in their natural state; it is man's work which gives them their value, when he sets about putting them at the service of society. From the logical point of view, then, things—or let us call them merchandise—ought to belong only to those who so transform them. Marx had a mere smattering of ethnology, but he went on boldly to say that in primitive societies such a state of affairs had really existed. The chief crime of capitalism lay in the divorce between work and ownership, for ownership became the prerogative of those who did not work at all, while the workers owned nothing and were forced to transform their own powers of work into merchandise, and to get very little for doing so.

If one has no major objection to the principal Marxist thesis, which claims that labour creates values, its fundamental theory, the pivot of the whole system, presents no further difficulties. Marxism is, indeed, a well-constructed system, whose various parts are all firmly articulated. The theory of surplus value explains all the workings of capitalistic society and proves it to be basically unjust, for it is founded on one man's exploitation of another and kept going only by lies and violence.

The capitalist has seized the gifts of nature and had them turned into merchandise by getting other men to work instead of working himself. These other men began by being slaves, then became serfs, and are now the workers. They have nothing to put on the market in exchange for the goods they must have if they are to live, and therefore have no choice but to sell their powers of work. According to Marx, the fundamental crime of capitalism is that the worker does not receive the *whole* reward of his work; at the time when he wrote, a worker's pay was only the equivalent of what it had taken him six hours to produce, whereas he worked twelve hours out of the twenty-four. This meant that capitalism cheated him of all the values which he had created during the second half of the day; and it is precisely this which constitutes "surplus value." It is to the capitalist's advantage to making working hours as long as possible: this is the simplest way of increasing surplus value. True, say his disciples, Marx never knew the latest stage of capitalistic evolution. The capitalist of today does not prolong working hours; instead, he speeds up the rate of production. But this does not affect the condemnation on principle of a system which produces surplus value. As Marxists see it, the entire fortune of a capitalist is always made by robbing the workers. In his own theoretical and abstract way, Marx took over the famous slogan of Proudhon: "Property is theft."

THE CONDEMNATION OF PRIVATE PROPERTY

Logically enough, Marx concludes from his analyses that private property was "at one time" legitimate—at a time, that is, before there was any divorce between capital and labour. Even today it is still legitimate for the artisan, and the peasant with a small holding. But both artisan and peasant are anachronistic survivals from a bygone age, fated to be driven out of existence by large-scale industry and vast agricultural enterprises. Marx had nothing but scorn for such moralists as the utopian socialists. His own condemnation of private property in capitalist society had nothing to do with morals. He was very much a man of the nineteenth century, and the prestige of such writers as Ricardo and Adam Smith greatly influenced him; the only solid social reality he believed in was economic. He held it to be a fundamental and self-evident truth that the whole existence of men and of human societies is inexorably determined by their economic conditions. We shall come back to this later. For the moment, I have only referred to this principle to make the Marxist condemnation of private property intelligible

Marx rejected the principle of private property because he thought it completely unsuited to modern methods of production. All the disorders of society—the destitution of some, the riches of others, unemployment, crises, intellectual and moral turmoil—all this was caused by the fact that the methods of production had changed, while the method of appropriation was still what it had been when it was meeting the economic needs and conditions of the artisan and small-scale peasant owner.

To Marx it seemed obvious that the primitive social order, and even feudalism, were "better" than capitalism. He went so far as to say that the thirteenth century was the "golden age of the workers." But one should not be misled as to the true meaning of such statements. All that the founder of scientific socialism meant when he said this is that at one time there was a perfect correspondence between the methods of production and of appropriation; he did not in the least mean that the men of those times were "happier" than the men of today. In capitalist society, the exploitation of one man by another is inevitable. This explains the contempt with which Marxists regard all theories and efforts which attempt to sugar-coat the pill of capitalism, to soften and improve it. I need hardly say that they have no thought of a possible return to a primitive or feudal form of society. We cannot, and rightly cannot, destroy our machines; it is neither possible nor even desirable to put the clock back, to resist the inevitable and necessary advance of technical progress. The means of appropriation must be adapted to the new means of production—not the other way around. And as, in modern economy, the means of production can only be collective, nothing but collective property will meet the present needs of society.

We must be careful to bear in mind that Marxism is only interested in the ownership of means of production. True, I myself and many other young middle-class Communists liked to picture a future Communist society where no one owned anything, where everything belonged to everybody. But in this we were thinking, not of the "social science" of Marxism, but of utopian socialism—or even of the ideal which inspired the first followers of Christ. Marxism itself by no means forbids, in a Communist society, the individual ownership of such goods as do not serve production. The State has merely to see to it that no one, by more or less devious methods, manages to get into his hands the instruments of production.

Like many other people, I paid but little heed to the perfectly clear distinction which Marxist doctrine draws between ownership of means of production and ownership of consumer goods. As only the former interested him, Marx, in his works on property, saw no point in stressing each time that he was not talking about the ownership of consumer goods. This made it possible for us, in good faith, to extend the collectivist ideal to ownership of all goods. As often happens, I had studied Marx with the unconscious wish to find in him the theoretic—we called it "scientific"—justification of my personal Communism, which was fundamentally far more effective than rational. What did I care about conformity between methods of production and methods of appropriation of the means of production! It all seemed so terribly abstract. On the other hand, I did care very much about finding some way of putting an end to the glaring inequalities that exist between men. To me, Communism was first and foremost the re-establishment of a living equality between human beings. At that time I had not heard the word "existentialism," but by my own outlook and spontaneous reactions I was already an existentialist. The one thing that really interested me was the concrete human reality; purely theoretical and abstract speculations never meant much to me. I was a Communist because I believed that Communism was going to make men happier. It was in the light of this ideal that I read and interpreted the works of Marx, Engels, Lenin and the other "theoreticians" of Communism.

DIALECTICAL AND METAPHYSICAL MATERIALISM

Every Marxist has necessarily to be a materialist. This must be taken in the fullest sense of the word—not in the interpretation put on it by certain Christian Communists, who want to see Marxist Communism as merely a way of explaining social developments by the predominance of economic factors. Some years ago the Italian Communist Elio Vittorini wrote that, on the philosophical level—when, that is, he wants to define his position as to the nature of things—a Communist can be, according to choice, a Kantian, a Bergsonian or a follower of Croce. Maurice Merleau-Ponty even did his best to reconcile Communism with existentialism. There is nothing in the traditions or principles of Communism to justify such eclectic tolerance. "To Hegel," we read in *Das Kapital,* "the thought-process, of which, under the name of 'idea,' he makes an autonomous subject, is the creator of reality. . . . To me the world of ideas is only the material world transposed and translated into the human mind." Nothing could be clearer; and it was in this dogmatic sense that my friends and I understood Marxist materialism. We believed with Engels that "the ideas of our brains are only more or less abstract copies of real objects and phenomena." To me, as to Marx and Engels, the words "real" and "material" were perfect synonyms.

There is no word which a Communist utters with such scorn as "idealism." He uses it to include more than those systems classified as idealist in histories of philosophy—Kant's, Hegel's, Renouvier's, Brunschvicg's. Like Engels, who established a radical heterogeneity between Hegel and Feuerbach, the Marxist divides the philosophers of all ages into categories—the idealists and the materialists. Aristotelian realism, the Christian spirituality of St. Augustine, Thomas Aquinas and Maurice Blondel, Cartesian rationalism, the positivism of Comte, Bergsonian vitalism, existentialism—all alike were labelled idealist. I should have found myself hard put to it to give a philosophically valid definition of such "idealism." We pushed pellmell into the same basket every philosophy which put ideas above matter, the absolute above the contingent; or which explained the universe as coming from a transcendent principle. After all, whatever form it took, idealism could only be a reactionary, and therefore false, philosophy. Nothing but materialism was progressive, and therefore true.

In imitation of my masters, I divided materialism into two categories—"common" materialism, as taught by Marx's predecessors, and "scientific" materialism. Although the latter stood incomparably higher, I concurred with all other Marxists in regarding the early materialists as forerunners—men who had had some shadowy presentiment of the truth. Only the genius of Karl Marx, however, had been up to discovering it as it really was; and from his day onwards it was his scientific materialism alone that knew all the answers.

Everyone who denied the primacy of spirit over matter was held to be a materialist. Matter alone was real; spirit was just an epiphenomenon—a sort of secretion of matter. In the history of philosophy, therefore, I felt it my duty to uphold Democritus, Epicurus and Lucretius rather than Plato or Plotinus: Francis Bacon, Hobbes and Locke rather than Descartes, Pascal and Leibniz. But above all I felt called upon to admire the French Encyclopedists of the eighteenth century. I had not, I need hardly say, actually *read* Holbach, Condillac or Diderot. But as Marx had been pleased to hail them as the masters of his thought, who was I to do otherwise? And Marx said that he owed even more to Ludwig Feuerbach, whom Engels praised as the man who had "put materialism firmly back on the throne" after the long eclipse into which the excesses of the French Revolution had plunged the Encyclopedists. Marx, it is true, said that Feuerbach was wrong in trying to find happiness for the individual. But this heresy was forgiven him, for having been the first person to attempt the materialistic transposition of Hegelian dialectic.

It went down well to praise the "mechanistic" materialism of those who came before Marx, but it would have been out of the question for anyone still to profess it after the full flood of enlightenment which Marx had brought with him. We Marxist intellectuals had one or two points in common with Christians as far as our mental attitude went, for Christians admire certain religious teachings and practices which existed before Christ, or even which still exist in countries to which the gospel has not penetrated But once the gospel is known, it seems inconceivable that people should still go on believing in the *Vedas,* Buddha or Zarathustra. In the course of this book, we shall come across other parallels between Marxist and religious dogmatism.

What did I, a materialist, understand by matter? Like every Marxist of the Communist obedience, I believed that all our ideas are the exact reflections of extra-mental material objects; in Engels' striking phrase, "our consciousness, our thought, however transcendent they may appear, are only the product of a material, corporeal organ— the brain." We believed that no criteriology was necessary to test the truth of our ideas; all one had to do was remain in constant touch with the material world. This contact with the material world—in other words, with "reality"—could only be brought about in and through human action. I think this conviction had a great deal to do with the fact that I myself became a man of action, in spite of my natural temperament.

"The materialism of the last century," wrote Engels, "was, above all, mechanistic, because at that time, of all the natural sciences, only mechanics, and, of that, only the mechanics of solid and earthly bodies—the mechanics of weight, in fact—had reached any state of advancement. . . . This exclusive application of mechanics to the phenomena of nature, even the chemical and organic phenomena, in which, it is true, mechanical laws also operate, but where they are put in the background by laws of a higher order—all this imposes a peculiar narrowness which was, however, inevitable in that day of classical materialism."

All this is appallingly badly put, but one can see from it that, to Engels, the mechanistic materialism known as "common" was also, in its own way, "scientific." Its shortcomings were due to the inadequacies of contemporary science. Marx and Engels, in the nineteenth century, were familiar with the epoch-making discoveries of the biologists and naturalists, especially such men as Darwin and Lamarck; and they also knew of the discoveries recently made in physics and chemistry. Their concept of matter was thus far fuller and more subtle than any which the Encyclopedists could have.

Had I really been faithful to Marx and Engels' own attitude to their predecessors, I should have gone on to argue that Marxist materialism itself was "scientific" only in relation to the stage of scientific evolution which had been reached in Marx's day. Since 1883—the year of his death—the strides made by science were at least as great as those between the period of the Encyclopedists and of Marx himself. New disciplines, of which he had no idea, have arisen —psychoanalysis, to name only one. I should, to be logical, have adopted the same critical attitude towards Marxist materialism which its author adopted towards his forerunners. But neither I nor any of the others ever thought of doing so.

With great disloyalty to the spirit of their master, twentieth-century Marxists continue to cling to a concept of matter which true scientists have long ago discarded. And, even if Marx's materialism could legitimately be called scientific, that of my comrades and myself certainly was not. Matter, which we regarded as the origin and principle of everything, assumed, in our eyes, a mysterious character which we never cared to define too closely. Communist scholars, in the Soviet Union as elsewhere, try to make out that Marxism always conforms to "science"; but how can they possibly do so, unless they twist the facts? I am amazed now that neither I nor other Marxist intellectuals ever saw that our idea of matter was not scientific at all, but purely metaphysical—using the word in the highly unfavourable sense which Marxists always give it. For, to them, any system is metaphysical which is founded solely on the gratuitous assertions of reason, completely divorced from contact with reality. I opted for materialism simply because I was a Communist Like many others, I never dreamed of testing the foundations which supported the "scientific" materialism whose dogmas I professed. This attitude was, of course, quite unscientific, and I must indeed have been blinded by my Communist *faith,* since for so many years I never saw it.

Like all my comrades, I was terrified of falling into heresy, and did not dare to look too closely at what the Party taught. We would not, for anything, have expressed whatever admiration we might feel for some form of philosophy whose "materialism" had not been vouched for by the higher powers. I myself, when I first started reading Bergson, was immediately captivated by his style, his soaring flights of thought, and the scrupulous care he took to do justice to the finest shades of reality. But I knew that official specialists in Party ideology had listed him among the most dangerous "idealists." In an attempt to justify the strong attraction his work had for me, I wrote a long article for a Marxist review, in which I tried to prove the "implicit materialism" of Bergson's philosophy. But for all my dialectical skilfulness, the article never appeared In my own heart, however, I never lost my admiration for Bergson, and some years later this was to be a great help to me.

All the time I was within the Marxist orbit, I was never able to make any really clear-cut distinction between Marxism as a *materialistic metaphysic,* with its claims to "scientificity," and Marxism as a dialectic, a method of explaining the development of human societies. When, therefore, I later broke with the Party I was tempted to make a clean sweep of everything that bore the Marxist label. It was not until 1948, when I started writing *Le Marxisme, Philosophie ambiguë et efficace,* that I came to see the modicum of truth contained in Marxism.

THE HEGELIAN ORIGINS OF MARXISM

Lenin tells us that it is impossible to be a good Marxist without a thorough knowledge of Hegel's philosophy; acting on this, I made a conscientious study of it for years. At a first glance, Marx would seem the exact opposite of the German idealist, who worshipped German imperialism, and whom Hitler claimed, with some reason, as the inspiration of his own *Weltanschauung.* But when I had made a more profound study of both Marx and Hegel it was borne in on me that Marx owed more to his master than Marxists, with their naïf wish to make him out as a sort of creator *ex nihilo,* are willing to admit. Even Marx himself, at least in his early days, seems not fully to have realized how close the bond was between them.

Hegel's speculations on the adventures of the absolute mind had fascinated Marx when he was a young student in Berlin, though he came later to speak of them with bitter contempt as a dangerous mystification and utter absurdity. At that time he was inclined to throw Hegel overboard and give himself up completely to the materialist tradition of philosophy. But a careful reading of his writings as a young man showed me that he never really shook off the spell which Hegel had cast over his youth. In after years he ceased to be a shamefaced Hegelian; he adopted dialectic openly and consciously. "In Hegel," he wrote in *Das Kapital,* "dialectic is walking on its head; one has only to stand it the right way up to see that it is quite reasonable."

Marx thought that he had succeeded in this operation of standing dialectic the right way up, by exchanging Hegel's idealistic notion of a *universal individual* for the materialistic notion of man as real and empirical. Whereas Hegel was only interested in a purely phenomenological development, unfolding within the mind, Marx

applied the method to the historical development of concrete humanity. Or this, at any rate, was how I then understood it. Later, when
I was used to a more severely critical form of philosophic thought, I
came to see that Marxist man was no more concrete than Hegelian
man, and that Marx's originality lay more in words than in things.

By reducing the real to the rational, Hegelianism had become a
philosophical justification of the established order, a kind of theoretical foundation for the Prussian State. Marxism did not, indeed,
deny the Hegelian premisses. But it did deny all rationality, and
hence all the prerogatives of reality, to the established order—
capitalistic society, founded as it was on chaos and economic contradictions. Moreover, it gave a revolutionary interpretation to that
other Hegelian principle which affirms that all things are relative.
This principle suited me down to the ground as long as it was a
question of destroying capitalism. But I found myself in difficulties
whenever, in discussions with intellectuals, I tried to defend the
definitive character of the revolution; for needless to say I did not
regard Communism itself as relative.

The methodical, even systematic, application of Hegelian dialectic
to social happenings struck me as ingenious, for it seemed to give a
complete coherence to all the events of history. In the lectures on
elementary Marxism which I gave to innumerable study groups, I
always greatly enjoyed quoting the illustration which Engels gave to
throw light on the famous law of Hegelian dialectic—the change
from quantity to quality. When hot water is put in a cold place, its
temperature goes down from 100 to 20, then to 15, then to 10; these
are all quantitative changes, for the substance itself remains water
throughout. The change becomes qualitative only when the temperature sinks below zero and we have, no longer water, but ice. The
Marxist application of this is as follows: in capitalistic society, the
parliamentary tussles carried on by liberals and progressives to
introduce various legal reforms are quite incapable of producing
any but quantitative changes in the established order, for this order
is fundamentally wrong, and can never be anything but wrong,
founded as it is on the appropriation of labour by capital. As in the

case of water, quantitative changes can lead on to qualitative changes, but these always take place suddenly, as a complete break with the old order of things. So Hegel encouraged me in my condemnation of "reformist" socialism. Nothing but the Communist revolution would ever be able, dialectically, to bring about a new world, as different from the old as ice from water.

Another dialectical law, that of the negation of negation, explained why the advent of Communism was inevitable not only morally but, if I may say so, physically. Without delving too far back into history, I used to show that medieval feudalism appeared to be the dialectic affirmation, or, if one prefers it, the *thesis*—whereas in reality it was already the negation of the old system based on slavery. Modern capitalism is the negation, the antithesis, of feudalism. Communism, which will abolish the division of society into mutually antagonistic classes, is the negation of the capitalistic negation, the supreme and final synthesis.

ECONOMIC SUBSTRUCTURES

The Marxist should, above all, be able to explain dialectically the economic relations between the members of any given society; if he cannot, his dialectic will not be of much avail, since, as we know, fundamental material reality, to him, is and continues to be, economic.

When Marx substituted economic categories for the logical categories of Hegel, he thereby claimed to demonstrate the dynamic nature of the essential social bond, the division of labour. There are many economic categories; only their sum total allows any rational reconstitution of the modern world as a concrete whole. Every epoch, however, is characterized by the predominance of one economic category or another. Capitalistic society, for instance, can find an explanation of all the principles it professes and all the values it stands for, in the category of *exchange value*. It is hardly surprising that Marx devoted several chapters of *Das Kapital* to this arid subject.

In primitive society, say the Marxists, the only value that any object possessed was its utility value, founded on the concrete relationship between economic wealth and man's needs. With the introduction of the division of labour—in itself a great step forward—men no longer produced commodities for their use alone, but for others, just as those others in their turn met certain needs of theirs. The product of labour thereby acquired, in addition to its utility value, an exchange value. In relation to merchandise, the two values are to be seen as two *dialectical moments in opposition.* The exchange of merchandise is, then, the dialectical negation of the isolation of individuals and social groups; it continuously forms new and concrete bonds between men and nations. This in turn will give way to a new form of human solidarity, concrete as the religious and patriotic myths of the past could never be. Objectively, then, trade economy should be regarded as marking a step forward in social life, an advance on the time when everyone produced goods only for himself and his family. The division of labour, which is the criterion of social progress, is thus built on vast foundations, for each individual is now working for society as a whole. But trade economy is unable to create universal harmony. Its internal contradictions give rise to a new economic category—competition—which leads to appalling conflicts between individuals and nations.

The second crime of trade economy is to turn—dialectically, as usual—the concrete labour of the artisan-worker into the abstract labour of the industrial worker. From the economic angle, the worker at this stage ceases to exist as a man; he only counts as an abstract and anonymous labour force. From the individual's point of view, this is deplorable, and Christian sociologists are much concerned by the problem. The Marxist, on the other hand, has to learn to disregard all "sentimental" considerations. He can only note that the industrial division of labour increases, quantitatively, the production of merchandise—which, qualitatively, should prepare the way for a more advanced form of social life. True to his Hegel, he always rates the general above the individual. In the modern world, ruled by trade economy, it would, he thinks, be foolish, useless and anachronistic to worry about the problems and interests of the individual. This explains the contempt we all felt for individual psychology based on introspection; we regarded it as an utter waste of time and used to jeer at people who sat "contemplating their navels" when the whole world needed changing. With these bracing principles, we had no pity whatever for the men and women in Russia who each day were ground beneath the wheels of advancing revolution; the horrifying stories of Soviet prisons and labour camps which poured from the press left us completely cold. In the same way, it seemed to us perfectly natural that we ourselves, when the time came, should die in the cause of the revolution, before we could even catch a glimpse of the promised land. This, at any rate, is the principle to which we all gave intellectual assent. In the secret places of those hearts whose existence we denied, we were all slightly more concerned with our own fate than we made out.

Before my conversion to Communism, aesthetic values were the only ones I prized. I didn't, therefore, find it at all easy to bring myself to say that in economic society the only real bonds between people were economic relations—production, buying and selling, money and contract. Our masters foresaw our objections and had their answer ready; as far as appearances went, economic conflicts and contradictions only existed between competing forms of merchandise. But, in the world of objective merchandise, man is no more than a pawn, an almost wholly passive tool; and every man, whether he wants it or not, finds himself swept into the *danse macabre* of trade. This economic activity, which works according to its own inherent laws—not as man tries to direct it, but as dominating man himself—is what Marx called "fetichism." Economic fetichism, like the magic of primitive peoples, brings man to his knees before material forces. He has the illusion of being able to organize the world, of being the master of his own work and its products But all that in fact he does is to carry out the ineluctable laws of the dialectical development of economy—which means that he is the mere slave of the merchandise he creates. Most men are unaware of their state of bondage. They think that the economic laws governing the capitalist world are natural laws, expressing the will of some providence or other. In obedience to Marx and Lenin, we waged a relentless war against this *mystified conscience*

As a Marxist intellectual, I had the proud feeling that I was fighting for higher aims than just to get a little more food for the poor; I was fighting also—chiefly, in fact—to destroy this mystified conscience; and my mission seemed to me extremely noble. Whatever I could do to help to destroy a capitalist society based on trade values would be at the same time a blow struck for the victory of a more advanced dialectical *moment*. No Marxist, of course, could hope that, once the capitalist structure of social relations had collapsed, each man would again become the master of his own work and its products. To us, capitalism was not just negativity in the usual sense of the word, but the dialectical negation of a state which was, objectively, inferior. The "mystification" against which we waged war had once been a historical necessity, to break up the old individualist economy. If capitalism had not achieved its objective aim, we should not now have the conditions indispensable to the triumph of the definitive synthesis of socialist economy. The trained Marxist must put every ounce of his strength into the fight against capitalism, but he must do so without any hatred or violent feelings. He must be able, dispassionately, with "scientific" objectivity, to explain its internal contradictions—periodic crises, unemployment, class warfare, and the rest.

A VISION OF THE WORLD AS A WHOLE

Many people find it impossible to understand how Communism has obtained the hold it has over so many highly educated men and women. Not only young students, but well-known writers and scholars announce that they are Marxists, and we have no reason to doubt their sincerity. Even the middle classes can understand why workingmen, "jealous" of those set over them, or down-and-outs whose one idea is murder and theft—why people such as these should turn Communist. But it seems paradoxical, or even just plain senseless, for graduates of advanced centres of learning to go the same way, though their level of education and, often, their social position, might be expected to keep them on the side of the privileged classes. In many cases, dark hints are dropped about "Russian gold"—which seems to make it quite unnecessary to search for any deeper explanation. But the most gullible of anti-Communists would hardly use this argument against such men as Joliet-Curie, Professor Haldane and Picasso, who, even in a capitalist society, are by no means kept short of money or honours. As far as their own interests are concerned, Communism has brought them no advantages at all— only very frequent, and often very serious, setbacks.

Many intellectuals, especially those from the middle classes, become Communists for idealistic or sentimental reasons, more or less as I did. But the reasons are relatively unimportant. As soon as they are Party members, almost all of them accept, apparently without much question, the Party concept of the world and existence. We must, then, recognize that, however easy it may be theoretically to pick holes in Marxist philosophy, it seems to satisfy them.

If we are to understand the Communist intellectuals, we must look for deeper and more serious explanations than Russian gold or a supposed complex of destruction. We must keep in mind the collapse of that unity which distinguished Western medieval civilization, and of which our great cathedrals are the symbol. Religion, science, art, individual and collective life, all made up a perfect whole, which satisfied man's deep-seated longing for unity. But this unity, founded on Christianity, broke down no less through the internal contradictions of a civilization centred too exclusively in the sacred, than through the scientific discoveries of modern days.

In the early stages, at about the time of the Renaissance, the sight of the rigid medieval unity lying in ruins seemed to fill people with an intoxicating sense of freedom. In every field—painting, sculpture, poetry, music, philosophy, even mysticism—the prevailing anarchy led to the creation of countless masterpieces. In later centuries, the freedom to question all recognized values, to go where the fancy takes one, has been chiefly of service to scientific research.

Man's discoveries, both geographical and scientific, the heightened creativity that was his, now that he had cast off his bonds—all this made the world larger and more complex. Unfortunately, however, it now had no centre, no pivot around which the various elements could coalesce and form a whole. Everything was scattered and dispersed; in fact, the position was very like that which followed the collapse of the Tower of Babel. The result, to nearly every educated Westerner, was a gnawing sense of insecurity. In the affective sphere it led to neurosis, the complaint typical of an inwardly disintegrated humanity. In the intellectual field it gave rise to eclecticism, which inevitably fails to satisfy any critical mind, and which, moreover, often leads to neurosis.

Anyone who has studied philosophy at any university in any Western country will undoubtedly understand and agree with what I have just said. In every university, several professors, simultaneously or successively, teach philosophy to twenty-year-olds. Most of these professors have, unquestionably, very good minds. Some declare themselves adherents of one or other school of philosophy; others either have their own system which they expound to their students, or show complete detachment from all systems and schools and simply take from each what they feel to be of value. One can imagine the effect of such teaching on the young, who have set out to study philosophy with the more or less explicitly conscious desire to know the truth. At the end of their studies they are logically forced to the conclusion, either that truth does not exist, or that there are as many truths as there are philosophies. Even if some of them do adopt one or other of the various systems, it is usually more for aesthetic than for purely philosophic reasons. But most of them resign themselves to becoming sceptics. And almost exactly the same problem faces the other students, who are reading history, science and so on. In all of them, systems and theories challenge, contradict, and cancel each other out. How is any young man to find in them that total truth which is the natural need of his mind?

Some claim that they satisfy this need with scepticism—the essential relativity of all values. One used to come across such people in the cafés of Montmartre and Montparnasse; now one sees them haunting the famous "cellars" round Saint-Germain-des-Prés. Their scepticism is only the more or less successful disguise of their neurosis. Those whose ego has something solid behind it reject scepticism and neurosis and set out valiantly to find that unifying principle of their existence which official teaching has failed to give them. Christian faith, authentic and understood on an adult level, may well become the pivot they need. But what help is there for young people whose family background and school education have been so wholly divorced from Christianity that they would never dream of turning to it in the hopes of finding an answer to their anguished questionings? Marxism apart, there is nothing, literally nothing, which can weld into one coherent whole their own lives, the universe about them, and the scientific and philosophic knowledge they have acquired. True enough, once one has adopted Marxism as the nucleus of one's *Weltanschauung* one finds that one has to give up not only the delights of anarchy, but—almost always—one's intellectual freedom as well. This is quite certainly the hardest sacrifice that Communism asks of intellectuals; but they themselves recognize its necessity, if their egos are not to disintegrate completely. It was not until I had made a prolonged study of depth psychology that I could understand my own unconditional surrender to Marxism, whose philosophical flaws I could have spotted so easily. Like most of my comrades who were intellectuals, what I needed was a faith, and Marxism did duty for one.

For Marxism claims to be more than a mere economic and political system; it claims to have a complete and satisfying answer to all human problems. Nothing is beyond its province—not history, not science, not art, nothing lies outside the territory which it claims as its own. Any aspects of reality which will not yield to its terrifyingly simple explanatory principles are contemptuously thrown aside. This gives all Marxists, even the most learned, an intellectual gullibility which astounds anyone who is in the habit of speculating on the mysteries of existence, or thinking with any degree of precision. But Marxists firmly believe that this ruthless elimination of all superfluous problems—all the frills, so to speak—increases their power of action. They have reverted, under the impulse of Marxism, to that medieval outlook against which the Renaissance took up the cudgels in the name of freedom of thought. Education, in Communist countries, sets out with the express purpose of training specialists—it can point to some noteworthy examples!—and has nothing but scorn for the "humanities"—that general culture which in Western Europe is regarded as all-important for the development of a complete personality.

MARXIST "SCIENCE"

Like all Marxists, I had the liveliest admiration for "Science." Religious people write the word "God" with a capital; to us it was "Science" which had to have a capital. The only truth that could exist was "scientific" truth; only "scientific" arguments held water in our discussions.

Yet I don't think our concept of science was entirely that of a twentieth-century scientist. We had taken over, fairly uncritically, the prevailing idea of the nineteenth century—Science as Marx and Engels had seen it. Science, to them, was in opposition to theological and metaphysical explanations, just as truth is in opposition to myths and mystification. The scientists of our day are more modest. Even with the vastly improved instruments at their disposal, they no longer dream of attaining complete and final truth. They have dropped the capital letter, and speak of "the sciences" rather than of "Science."

Clinging as we did to a concept of Science which the sciences reject, we had unconsciously adopted exactly that intellectual attitude which Marx had denounced as metaphysical. We loudly proclaimed that Marxist dialectic was Science, and that the value of the other sciences lay entirely in their subordination to materialist dialectic. Now Hegel's dialectic is concerned only with eternal ideas. Our

Marxist dialectic was held not only to impart a perfect knowledge of the material world—the *real* world—but also to be the best possible tool for transforming it. Here again we were, without knowing it, following the scholastics whom post-Cartesian philosophers so heartily despise. The scholastics, too, believed that there was one supreme Science with which the experimental sciences had nothing in common. This was metaphysics. With us, dialectic held exactly the same place that metaphysics had held with the scholastics; it was the touchstone, the guarantee of truth, of all the other sciences.

Dialectic materialism enabled one (we held), in the scientific knowledge of *reality,* to attain results at least as impressive as those achieved by Hegelian dialectic in the field of phenomenology of the mind. Even Engels, as far back as his day, said that the most important scientific discoveries had been made by applying—often unconsciously—dialectical materialism. The discovery of the cell as a unity, the conservation of energy, Darwin's theory of the evolution of species, and so forth, were all, according to him, traceable to this use of dialectic. I wasn't, of course, up to testing the truth of these statements; but they chimed in admirably with my idea of Marxism. I lost no time in appropriating these notions of Engels' and extending them to other fields.

Being a good Marxist, I could not ascribe scientific progress to human genius alone; like everything else, it was inevitably determined by the development of the means of production. Why, the learned English Marxist, J. B. S. Haldane, said as much in his book *Marxist Philosophy and the Sciences.* Astrology originated in the need of primitive races to calculate important annual events in order to ensure their food supply; they wanted to know the time of the lambing season, for instance, or the rise of the Nile. From this they went on to draw up a calendar, which led in its turn, through various other economic necessities, to the most complex arithmetic. Land surveying gave rise to geometry; artillery problems brought in the study of ballistics; the study of ballistics ended in Newton's discovery of dynamism. We even went the lengths of fathering on dialectical materialism the quantum theory, and all modern chemistry and physics. In fact, we thought we had discovered in certain cryptic utterances of Engels' the prediction—not a *prophetic* prediction, a *scientific* one— of all scientific discovery and invention yet to be.

Where biology was concerned, Darwin's teaching on the evolution of species was a cardinal truth which no one was allowed to question. We refused, of course, to divide "nature" into the biological, on the one hand, and the chemical and mechanistic, on the other. Marxist condemnation of Bergson was, indeed, occasioned by his assertion that the vital could not be reduced to the mechanical. It is true that, at the same time, though for precisely opposite reasons, Bergson was causing perturbation among the Catholics, who feared that his "vitalism" could not be reconciled with authentic spirituality. Today, when the true essence of his philosophy has been clearly stated in *Deux Sources de la Morale et de la Religion,* one has to admit that the Marxists were far more clear-sighted over him than the Christians. For it was not spirituality but materialism which his philosophy was to shake to its foundations.

The most difficult thing of all to dialectize was psychology. To keep the Marxist structure of human knowledge intact, we had to start by jettisoning, as unscientific, all suggestion of the irrational, which we regarded as a mere nonsensical survival of the primitive mentality. Civilized man, as Marxists conceived him to be, acts solely on rational lines; seen from this standpoint, the psychological side of him can only be a shade further evolved than the physiological. This meant that the only psychology that we were free to acknowledge was one that could be reduced to physiology and thus, finally, to chemistry and mechanics. Lenin had, indeed, no great right to talk about psychological matters, but in my various lectures and articles I always liked to bolster myself up with one of his sayings: "The elimination by materialism of the 'mind-body' dualism consists in the assertion that the mind has no existence apart from the body, for mind is only a secondary factor, a function of the brain, a reflection of the exterior world."

In my passion to explain everything in the light of Marxist dialectic there was, no doubt, some need to reassure myself. How could I, indeed, have failed to see, at least from time to time, the depth and beauty of some philosophy which I had to study at the university?

HISTORICAL MATERIALISM

However important I might consider the application of Marxist dialectic to biology, mechanics and physics, I was quite aware that its real function was to provide an explanation of social development. The day I joined the Young Communists, I did not undertake to do what I could to advance the natural sciences, but to transform society. In the scientific field I felt I was doing quite enough by repeating parrot-fashion the views officially held by the Party. Historical materialism, on the other hand, I really have studied deeply; and if I have ever made an original contribution to Marxist thought, it is in that sphere. The two theses I wrote for my doctorate both had historical materialism as their subject. In my major thesis I tried to show the originality of Marx's revolutionary dialectic in relation to Hegelian dialectic, and emphasized the outstanding part played by the former in the Revolution and construction of the Communist State in Russia, and in the international working-class movement. In my minor thesis I set out to demonstrate the superiority of the dialectical Communism of Marx and Lenin to the "static" communism of Plato.

My youthful excursions into philosophy were all aimed at proving that historical materialism was not just a theory of knowledge, as almost every philosophic system is content to be. It was, first and foremost, an instrument of social revolution. My partisan zeal certainly led me to exaggerate the originality of Marxism. Yet I ought to have known that even such typically "middle-class" historians as Guizot, Thiers and Michelet had taught that any history worthy of the name was not just—as school textbooks usually make out—a recital of dynastic, diplomatic and military events. They looked for the causes, and the material—even economic—conditions that lay behind such momentous happenings as the French, and later the English industrial, revolutions. Hegel himself, in his grandiose outline of universal history, spoke not only of political society—the State—but of economy as well. The only originality which I could with any justice ascribe to historical materialism was in so far as it regarded the facts and events which make up history as being mere *effects* of the economic conditions of any given human society. "Historical materialism," wrote Engels, "seeks the ultimate cause and main motive force of all important historical events in the economic development of society, in the changes taking place in methods of production and exchange, in the consequent division of society into separate classes, and in the struggles between these classes." This calls for a few comments.

To me it seemed perfectly obvious that human history, in the course of which tribes became States and one civilization and culture followed another, was the effect, the outcome, of the development of material living conditions—especially the means of production. I disassociated myself completely from those historians and sociologists who study the effect on history of climate, geological structure, or the more or less accidental changes which occur in animal or organic nature. Of course, I too did not wholly shut my eyes to these factors but, as a good Marxist, I concerned myself almost exclusively with the economic causes in history. Within the framework of historical materialism, I saw every society primarily as an entity producing economic wealth. In this too I was a faithful follower of Engels, who wrote: "The way in which men in any given society produce what they need, and then exchange the products among themselves, is the true characteristic of the history of society." Here again the Marxist crosses swords with Hegel, for Marxism holds that men do not make their own history or create States or civilizations to fulfil an idea or ideal which has dawned on them from some unspecified source of enlightenment; but solely to satisfy their material needs. It is for this, and this alone, that they invent tools, techniques and arts. Every economic advance inevitably brings with it some modification, greater or lesser according to circumstances, of social relations.

This "de-poetization" of history and life of course cost me something. The aesthete was not wholly dead in me. As often happens when the children of the upper middle class revolt against their natural background, I did not find it easy to rid myself of a certain contempt for economic realities, which seemed to me terribly lacking in dignity compared with the *free* activities of mankind—art, philosophy, science or even warfare. I had to tell myself that "human nature" itself was only the result of a certain organization of economic forces, within a civilization conditioned by these forces. Moreover, a true Marxist must never say that any social structure is good or bad "in itself." Even slavery was justifiable as long as it was in keeping with the productive capacity of its time. It was only when the productive capacity had evolved further that any given social structure could be said to be going against human nature. "Moralism" is, if possible, still more alien to historical materialism than aestheticism. Stalin was in the true Marxist tradition when he spoke of Ivan the Terrible as his forerunner—either forgetting or shutting his eyes to the bloodthirsty ferocity of his life. If Ivan the Terrible had been a contemporary, it is quite certain that he and Stalin would have been enemies. But he was as *necessary* to the Russian people of his day as Stalin was to become after 1925. The amorality of these views gave scandal to some idealists; but it was Stalin and not they who were faithful to the Marxist spirit. Even after my break with the Party, however, it took me years to see that this was so.

THE TREND OF HISTORY

My Marxist friends and I used often to debate whether economic factors—productive forces in particular—were or were not the one and all-sufficing cause of human history. Was it enough to know the productive forces of any given society to be able to decide with scientific precision what form of government, what methods of ownership, what culture, would suit it best? I myself felt slightly uncomfortable at having to profess such hard-and-fast determinism. I should have liked to make more allowances for individual initiative; above all, I should have liked to believe that in certain exceptional cases the thought and actions of "great men"—Lenin during the Revolution, for instance—had considerable bearing on the course of events. My fellow supporters of sociological determinism found innumerable passages in Marx, Engels and Lenin to quote at me, all proving how strongly coloured with "idealist" illusions my attitude was. Argument from authority is always unanswerable among Marxist Communists. I don't think any Christian or Mohammedan is so ready to discard his own critical faculty at the behest of a Scripture which he believes to be divinely inspired, as a Marxist confronted by the writings of his masters. In this again we were strikingly like the decadent scholastics of the fourteenth century. Our major concern was to turn up some passage in the writings of the official "doctors" of Marxism which would fit in with what we wanted to prove.

As to the question of historical determinism, it was Marx himself who answered it. "Are men free to choose their social framework?" he asked, and replied categorically: "By no means. Given a certain stage of development of production, commerce, consumption, and you will have a certain social constitution, organization of the family, of ranks or of classes: in short, a certain form of society." Moreover, man has but little control over the productive forces which so greatly affect his "destiny." He cannot continue as an artisan in the age of machinery; were he to insist on doing so, he would be ruthlessly trampled out of existence, and no Marxist would have the least pity for so fossilized a relic of the past.

I had no choice but to accept a thesis which had been overwhelmingly "proved" by the founder of "scientific" Communism; moreover, I could not fail to see that the doctrine of historical determinism gave our propaganda a particularly telling argument. I had been greatly struck, on reading Marx's life, by the story of his friend, the German poet, Heine. Heine was appalled by Communism, which he saw as the triumph of a mob of barbarians over the cultured few. But he was perfectly certain, from Marx's writings, that triumph it must; and the thought of it caused him hallucinations which brought him to the verge of madness. With this precedent in mind I used, in my discussions with young intellectuals, to make constant references to those theses of historical materialism which proclaim the inevitable victory of Communism. This really amounted to saying: "Since it can't be avoided, why try to oppose it? Wouldn't it be more sensible to go with the trend of History?"

We Marxists were the first to write the word "History" with a capital. We all of us believed that history had only one trend and that Communism alone was within that trend No matter what its enemies did, they could never prevent its triumph; the most they could do was delay it, or make its coming more painful than it need otherwise be. There was no question but that capitalism was done for; it was nothing now but an obstacle blocking the way against the advance of History. Any attempt to defend it against the attacks of the revolutionary proletariat would only prolong and intensify human suffering: only make the birth-pangs of the new order still more excruciating. I used, in many of my writings, to argue somewhat after this fashion: "To bring about a revolution is to behave like a good and compassionate surgeon. If a human limb has gangrene, medicine may help to prolong life or dull the pain, but it cannot save the patient from death. The less delay there is about amputating the limb, the greater his chances of recovery and the less he will suffer. Capitalist society, completely at odds with the present stage of productive power, is rotten through and through. Socialists who merely want reforms are like bad doctors, who aim at nothing more than causing some slight improvement. But we Communist revolutionaries are like surgeons at the top of their profession. We shall hurt only to bring about a quick and lasting cure."

My capacity for philosophic thought was not yet sufficiently mature and independent for me to realize that all our talk about the trend of History was in flagrant contradiction of a really materialist philosophy of history. I did not yet know that modern physics had recently shown that matter itself was less subject to determinism than to chance. As to History, it may be said to have a trend only when seen from the standpoint of either Christian eschatology or Hegel's idealist dialectic. Marxists claim to be materialists in their concept of history. In actual fact, here as in so many cases, they follow Hegel more closely than they realize. And in doing so they unwittingly abandon their materialism.

IDEOLOGICAL SUPERSTRUCTURE

I was not, any more than are other Marxists, credulous enough to see *only* the economic substructure of the complex social reality. In any case, the mere fact that we spoke of a substructure showed that we were not blind to what was built on top of it. How could I not have failed to know that, in addition to the forces of production and the system of commercial exchange, every form of society is characterized by activities such as art, music, literature, philosophy, law, religion and so on, which do not appear to be particularly "economic." Again, I could not overlook the fact that in every age and country there have been men who believed that they lived and died for ideas—not just for concrete economic realities. We ourselves, in our speeches and writings, would sometimes allude to the beauty and splendour of the "Communist ideal." Indeed, was it not that ideal, rather than any economic contradictions, that had made me a Communist?

With a frankness equalled by my good faith, I announced that "those ideological regions that float aloft in air" (Engels) were only *epiphenomena* of human productive activity. I tried, in one of my books, to "explain" Plato's philosophy by the economic conditions of fourth-century Greece; Kant and Hegel by the rise of capitalism; sculpture, and the paintings of Raphael, by mercantile economy. I firmly believed that the Communist economy of Russia would produce a completely new and specifically Communist type of music, painting, poetry, philosophy and science. On each of my visits to the Soviet Union (from 1929 onwards I made many) I kept an anxious watch for the first shoots of the cultural *epiphenomena* which must inevitably bloom from the subsoil of socialist economy. To my annoyance, I never saw anything but amateurish bunglings. I fully endorsed the many censures and excommunications hurled by the Central Committee at artists, scholars, scientists and philosophers

who still clung to "bourgeois" forms and methods. I consoled myself
with the thought that there was as yet no specifically socialist intellectual activity in the Soviet Union; the Communist regime had not
long been set up there, and Marx and Engels themselves had foretold
that the ideological superstructure of capitalism would not vanish
the moment socialist economy was introduced. It would take time for
this socialist economy to build new superstructures of its own. I was
to imagine the substructure, or subsoil, as an orchard, manured and
planted in a certain way, and destined to bear an ideological growth
of flowers and fruit, which, however, could not be expected to appear
until the trees had reached maturity.

I myself was responsible for several works of thought and imagination which I meant to be truly Communist, not only in subject but
in form. Between 1925 and 1934 I had quite a large output, but
everything I wrote was either a second-rate novel or a play-with-a-
purpose—all of it in the category of propagandist writing which,
unfortunately for literature, Communists are not the only people to
go in for, and which has never yet produced a masterpiece. I was
keenly aware of the failure of my attempt to help in the creation of a
Communist art, but being a Marxist I consoled myself with the
thought that I too belonged, both by birth and in the field of my
activities, to a social order riddled with corruption. Dialectically, it
would have been almost impossible for my work to be anything but
the continuation of the bourgeois substructure beneath it.

My own experience, then, did nothing to shake my belief that the
so-called independence of art and all ideologies from economic
factors was quite illusory. One could not, if one had any regard for
the truth, speak of an evolution or of an autonomous history of
philosophy, art, science and religion. As Marx wrote, "Men develop
their production and material trade, and while doing so create conditions for thought and the results of thought." But the transition from
the economic to the ideological substructure will take place not
mechanically but dialectically.

I knew, of course, that certain ideologies had revolutionized the
universe. The Christian ideal turned the Graeco-Roman world in-
side-out; then, at the end of the eighteenth century, the Christian

world was destroyed in its turn by the ideals of liberty and progress. Historical materialism, however, taught me to believe that this apparent victory of ideal was nothing of the sort, but a mere pretence and delusion. And there may I say in passing that from the Marxist point of view it is a pity that Communists so airily dismiss Freudian psychoanalysis, whose theories on various "disguises" might well provide them with useful arguments in support of the Marxist theory of superstructures. Moreover, there is nothing to prevent a Marxist psychoanalyst from explaining even the unconscious by economic substructures.

In any case, whatever points of resemblance there may be between Marxism and psychoanalysis, we Marxists held that the reason for the swift triumph of Christianity in the Roman Empire was the economic situation which had arisen at about that time. The old religious and philosophic ideologies (my knowledge of which was as skin-deep as it was of Christianity) were no longer *adapted* to the new economic conditions, and Christianity took their place without much difficulty. As for the ideals of liberty and progress, we held that their triumph was due entirely to the terrific technical progress of the last few centuries. Philosophic liberalism could not fail to be the ideological superstructure of free trade, and free trade was the inevitable outcome of improved means of production.

These theories, we thought, absolved us from having any feelings of awe towards those supposedly spiritual pseudo-values, the ideologies; for these were never either any worse or any better than their economic substructures. Since I condemned capitalism as an outworn economic system, I felt bound to condemn, equally strongly, the religion which tried to justify it, the principles it professed regarding individual freedom, and the private property on which it was based. In Marxism, everything hangs together.

THE INTERFERENCE OF CAUSES

Opponents of Communism are often amazed that the masses influenced by Communism remain almost impervious to anti-Communist propaganda, whose main line of attack is the fatal threat to personal freedom which Communism entails. Such anti-Communists usually know nothing whatever of the concept of freedom held by those who believe in historical materialism.

I am not, of course, saying that the working class as a whole is well up in all these Marxist speculations. None the less, at least some of the basic theses of historical materialism have been so widely publicized by the press, propaganda pamphlets and books, and speeches at trade union conferences, that the masses have, in general, come to accept them as fundamental truths—often enough, without suspecting their Marxist origins.

Marxism teaches that there is not, and never could be, any personal freedom for the proletariat within a capitalist society. What personal freedom can men have when they laboriously wrest their living from day to day, with no guarantee for the morrow, either for themselves or their families? The proletarian depends entirely on the whims of the capitalist. The "benefits of civilization," of which one hears so much, do not affect him; they were not made for him, and it is not in his interest to defend them. The middle-class aesthete may, if he likes, go into ecstasies over the freedom of the tramp; but working-men have rubbed shoulders too long with poverty to see anything "poetic" in destitution. The ruling classes have been clever enough to pass off as a self-evident truth what holds good only of the privileged. The one freedom worth anything—to the Marxist no less than to the proletariat—is collective freedom. This is identified with a social order which would make it impossible for one man to exploit another; would guarantee work, and therefore a living, to everyone; and give all alike equal opportunities for rising to any position they liked.

It was not till later that I saw how oversystematized, overlogical, these Marxist theses were. My chief concern at that moment must be not to oversimplify the explanations of social life which I preached for years—social life interpreted in the light of historical materialism. It was, of course, an article of my Marxist creed that ideologies were only the spiritual superstructures on economic substructures; but, like all reasonably well-educated Marxists, I knew it was not always easy to show how any given superstructure is logically based on its substructure. I didn't overlook the fact that ideologies affect not only each other but also the economic conditions of a people or a period. Religion often influences philosophy, but it influences the organization of production, too. An instance of this is the corporation of the Middle Ages. Philosophy affects art; art can guide technical research —and so on. If one race prefers a monarchy and another a republic, it is not necessarily because—in England, for example—the economic substructures favour the first form of government, and in France the second. The Marxist does not shut his eyes to the network of complex reciprocal influences, actions and reactions within any given society. It was in the Hegelian category of reciprocal action and dialectic change that I found the philosophic principles I needed in order to understand the interference of causes. But, like a good Marxist, I was quite sure that, even if I could not prove it in every case, in the final analysis it was possible to find a bond of causality between *all* spiritual superstructures and their economic substructures. It surprised me to learn later that the disciples of other schools of thought, with just as much conviction and apparent logic, relate everything to—let us say—some principle of metaphysics.

THE CLASS STRUGGLE AS A MOTIVE FORCE IN HISTORY

To use the Hegelo-Marxist terminology, I regarded economic conditions as constituting the first *moment* of the dialectic movement in the history of humanity. The second *moment*—that is, the dynamic factor which propels society on to progressively higher levels—is known as the class struggle. The division of society into classes, which are not only distinct but opposed, is the fundamental methodological postulate of historical materialism. We even used to insist that if one could imagine a state of affairs in which the division and opposition of classes did not exist, history would cease and mankind perish. We believed that the "scientific" foundation of this thesis lay in the famous Darwinian theory of the struggle for life and of natural selection.

The division of society into classes, as Marxists see it, has a strictly economic origin. With the introduction of specialized social functions which was the natural accompaniment of the division of labour, men or families with the same economic interests at heart formed themselves into groups, and in doing so brought into being mutually opposed classes or castes. As these classes are based on the antagonism of economic interests, the only possible relation between them is that of conflict. Though India is still split into endless rival castes, we held that, in the West, society had long since resolved itself into two principal and conflicting classes—the dominant and the oppressed. Right up to modern times, the dominant class, in which all power was vested, was the aristocracy. The middle class, it is true, was not the only one to be oppressed, but it stood in the van of economic progress and was therefore the most keenly aware of the privileges of the aristocracy. At that stage, then, with the objectivity which all Marxists pride themselves on, we regard the middle class as revolutionary and progressive. But as soon as it seized power it, too, lost no time in becoming reactionary and conservative; and from that moment onwards the only revolutionary class was the proletariat. Indeed, it plays its part with unrivalled excellence, for no other oppressed class in history has suffered so grievously from the tyranny of the dominant class.

The various forms which the class struggle takes on at different periods are determined by conditions of production. It is, of course, quite out of the question that the clock of technical progress should ever be put back, and this means that the victory of the progressive, revolutionary party over the conservative, reactionary party is a matter of sheer "dialectical" certainty. The final triumph of the proletariat is, then, assured by the irreversible nature of technical civilization. The economic structure of feudalism had been made obsolete by technical development, and middle-class domination was unable to cope with more than the first stages of this technical evolution. On the Marxist analysis, nothing but collective ownership could fit the structure of large-scale industry; and we refused to believe in the good faith of anyone who still stood up for capitalism. I felt an equal contempt for the "Utopians" who dreamed of going back to a pre-capitalistic, individualist economy. The attempts of some governments to encourage family ownership in agriculture seemed to us mere self-interested conservatism. Karl Marx had foretold that the concentration of industry and agriculture lay in the direct line of technical development. Our duty as Communists was to bring about the triumph of the revolution; the revolution in its turn would establish the one social order adapted to modern conditions of production —Communism.

To fan the sparks of class warfare by all the means in our power: to do everything possible to put a spoke in the wheel of any policy of conciliation and collaboration—all this gave us an intoxicating sense of working *within* the trend of History. We attacked reformist socialism and the Christian-Socialist movements even more acrimoniously than we attacked the forces of reaction, for we regarded them as the hangers-on of capitalism, whose attempts to improve working-class conditions within the existing social structure could only serve to prolong it. Nor had we any greater liking for working-class co-operative movements for production and consumption, and the like. It is true that our working-class comrades sometimes joined these organizations, but solely in order to do propaganda in them and, above all, to divert to the cause of the revolution some of the vast financial resources of the co-operative movements in certain countries—notably England and Germany.

The same held good as regards the strikes which the Communists organized or took part in. There, too, they had not the slightest interest in the immediate results; all they cared about was to heighten the tension of the class struggle. Sometimes they would even see to it that the strike did not lead to better pay, for they were afraid that improved conditions might make the workers satisfied with things as they were in the capitalist world. The examples of America and Scandinavia were anything but encouraging in this respect.

We Marxist theorists had one overriding duty—to enlighten working-class consciousness. The proletariat—using the word in the almost mystical sense which Marxists give to it—is not chiefly made up of men living in wretched conditions. Its essential element is *class consciousness*—a consciousness of the incurable antagonism between the dominant class—at present, the middle—and the proletariat. But it is also a consciousness of the absolute certainty that the proletariat will win. The good Marxist ought on principle to look at these problems coolly and dispassionately. In the books and articles I wrote on theory, I never ceased to point out (and in this I was only repeating the teaching of Marx, Engels and Lenin) that at a given stage of historical development, feudalism and capitalism were *right*. Marxism, however, is not content with being a purely descriptive philosophy; it is also out to further the cause of proletarian revolution. More important than any theoretical speculation about the past is the work of fostering antagonism between the classes. It was our duty, therefore, in everything that we wrote for the masses, to glorify "sacred class-hatred," though in so doing we were appealing to those affective motives which Marxism, with its wish to appeal only to the reason, despises. But once again, efficacy got the better of principle, and to us there could be no truth that was not efficacious. Perhaps I myself was even more fanatical than the others in stirring up hatred of capitalism; the resentment I felt against my early background had not yet been liquidated.

We were greatly worried over the situation in countries like the United States, Scandinavia, and even, to some extent, Great Britain. In the United States particularly, the development of capitalism had taken a turn which Marx had not foreseen. Technical progress and the concentration of industry and agriculture had there been carried further than anywhere in the world, and had still not led to a revolutionary situation. Instead of falling, as the Marxists had foretold, into progressively deeper poverty, the working class had, on the whole, shared in the general prosperity, and showed no wish to overthrow capitalism and bring in communism. The powerful trade unions did, indeed, organize strikes, but these had a strictly economic aim; they rejected the very principle of the class struggle, and made no secret of their hostility to Communism. And in Scandinavia the state of affairs seemed to us, if possible, even more scandalous. There, in fact, the prosperity of the workers, and their refusal to have anything to do with class warfare, was due to the systematic political reforms carried out by the socialist parties in power.

Great, then, was our joy when, in 1930, we learnt of the crash of the City banks—the first sign of the terrible economic crisis that was to have such appalling consequences in the United States and all other capitalistic countries. We never doubted that we should now see the fulfilment of Marxist predictions; that the United States and Scandinavia would no longer be spared the class struggle; and that the downfall of capitalism was at hand all over the world. Alas, once again our Marxist "science" let us down, for there followed instead the rise of Hitler in Germany, the arms race, and, finally, war.

SOCIALIST EMULATION

There was one point in particular on which the explanations of historical materialism failed to satisfy me. True, the picture it gave of social development was magnificent—almost as magnificent as the adventures of the Mind in Hegel's phenomenology. But, if class warfare was to be regarded as the chief, if not the only, motive force in History, what was to become of History once a classless society had arisen—a society which would wipe out all classes and, with them, the class struggle? Were we to believe that Communism would mean the end of historical development? I for my part was too thoroughly imbued with Hegelian dialectic to be able to imagine any end whatever to History.

I sought in vain for enlightenment in the writings of Marx, Engels and Lenin. They all showed the same coy reticence when it came to describing the dialectical structure of future Communist society. I put the question to a good many leading exponents of Party theory, especially in the U.S.S.R. They found it as embarrassing as I did. Most of them, afraid of getting onto dangerous ground and calling down on themselves the thunderbolts of the Politburo, evaded the issue and changed the subject. Others thought, as I did, that the coming of Communism could not possibly imply the end of History. Communism could never be fossilized into immobility; its development must continue to be governed by the laws of dialectic. The one solution, then, was to find a new motive force, a new second moment of the dialectic process.

This was later to become a very pressing problem, for Stalin and his staff, with an eye on external and internal propaganda, announced that the transition stage was now over and a classless Communist society was already established in the U.S.S.R. But would anyone have dared to claim that Russia round about 1935 had attained the final perfection of a Communist society and had no need of further progress, social, scientific or economic? Soviet citizens were far from enjoying a state of complete bliss, and the Russian reality bore no resemblance to what Communists in other countries expected from victory. There was still undoubtedly much to be done, and no Marxist could conceive of its being done otherwise than in accordance with the laws of dialectic.

It was at this point that Marxist-Leninists hit on the idea of presenting *socialist emulation* as the new form of dialectical *negation*. Men, even when they were delivered from all antagonism and no longer had anything to set them at loggerheads—even when they were perfectly aware of the trend and final goal of History—would still continue to fight. But it would not now be a case of men fighting *against* each other, only *with* each other. In this way, social progress could be dialectically guaranteed to go on for ever, and Communist society would reach a state of perfection which could be added to indefinitely. If the class struggle may be compared with war, socialist emulation might be likened to some competition in sport, in which men would fight, with the weapons of peace, for the sheer fun of the contest and the glory of winning. Again, where the class struggle fed on hatred of one's adversary, socialist emulation would thrive on the sense of solidarity between all members of a society which at last was free. Each man now would have only one ambition—to outstrip all previous efforts to serve Communist collectivity.

The Stakhanovism of the first Russian Five Year Plans was based on this concept of socialist emulation, and was also intended to be a concrete proof of the excellence of the theory. It would, however, be untrue to say that the theory itself entirely satisfied me on the intellectual plane. Moreover, as I shall show later, what was actually taking place in Russia did not at all come up to our expectations. But if my convictions were to remain intact, I had to have some kind of explanation, so I accepted the theory of socialist emulation without too much inward resistance. I even defended it in several articles that I wrote for reviews.

THE DICTATORSHIP OF THE PROLETARIAT

Both to myself and—even more—to others, I often felt called upon to explain and justify the state of dictatorship in the Soviet Union. Was not the revolution supposed to bring about the liberation of mankind?

During my visits to the U.S.S.R. I had seen this dictatorship in action, and found it hard to put aside the sense of uneasiness that it gave me. For a long time I tried to simplify the problem by deliberately clinging to the illusion that the Russian prisons and concentration camps were filled solely with enemies of the proletarian revolution—survivors of the old privileged classes, who wanted to sabotage the triumphant advance of the revolution. No Communist believes that one can wear kid gloves when one is conducting a revolution, and I was not quite so simple as to imagine that everyone would rush in overnight to do his part in building up the new social order. So I saw nothing to criticize in the harsh treatment that descended on the enemies of the proletariat.

But I could not shut my eyes to the obvious fact that the Communist dictatorship weighed heavily on even the most ardent militant Communists, and that the workers themselves were afraid of it. Again and again I heard that some comrade whom I had got to know on a previous visit to Russia had been sentenced to forced labour or deportation. His one crime was some deviation from the official, and endlessly revised, Party line—almost always over a matter of detail. Yet in every capitalist country the Communists carried on a brisk campaign against legal proceedings over questions of private opinion.

It was hard to find anything in Marx or Engels to justify the dictature of the proletariat as it existed in Soviet Russia. Lenin himself, in the early days of the Soviet regime, had favoured the principle of working-class democracy. He would have liked free discussion within the Party, and, in the beginning, even approved of a division of power among several working-class Parties.

As no better explanation was forthcoming, I told myself that the dictatorship of the proletariat had been found necessary in the Soviet Union because Russian workingmen and peasants were backward and had not, like the workers of the West, a long tradition of political and trades-union activity behind them. They were perhaps as yet unable fully to grasp the aims of the revolution, and this made them fall easy victims to the propaganda of the enemies of Communism. The revolution had so far triumphed in only one country, and the Soviet Union was hemmed in by hostile powers. This seemed to me quite to explain, if not justify, the Draconian methods of the dictatorship.

And no doubt it was true—but not the whole truth. So undeveloped was Russia, both technically and economically, that Marx had foretold that Communism would not come into power there until it had first triumphed in every country in Western Europe. The circumstances of history, and the political genius of Lenin, have disproved the predictions of the father of historical materialism, but without affecting the accuracy of his diagnosis. If Communism was to remain in power, it was essential for Russian economy to bring about a whirlwind transformation—a transformation such as it had taken Western capitalism a century to achieve Ordinary technical methods were quite unable to perform such a feat. The dictatorship of the proletariat, with its prisons and forced-labour camps, its trials for sabotage and its heresy hunts, became the motive force of socialist construction—a motive force which bore no relation to the *second moment* of the dialectical process. When I discovered all this, I was horrified; but I too toed the line.

MARXIST HUMANISM

Marxism, to me, was the science of social relations and of history, certainly. But it was something else as well—something, if possible, even greater. I cannot remember Communists using the term "Marxist humanism" as far back as between 1925 and 1935; yet it was the most important feature of all, at least where the intellectuals of the Party were concerned.

It was our claim that we could explain man and his problems by dialectics. More than this, however, we believed that we had an instrument by whose means we could remake him and create a new and better humanity. As the Soviet novelist, Ilya Ehrenburg, was later to write: "We shall transform men so thoroughly that they will hardly know themselves." There was something terrifying, something Promethean, in such an ambition.

Before the triumph of Communism, men had had only a *natural* history; their really *human* history would not begin until all the alienations of the human essence had been brought to an end. We could only pity such misguided people as "progressive" Christians, who refused to see any more in Marxism than an economic doctrine or a method of political action. Marxism, as the perfect and definitive *science,* must be the explanation of everything. It must above all be a humanism According to Marx, the chief crime of capitalism had been the alienation of the human essence: we naturally looked on the regeneration of this essence as the main object of the revolution. We had to dethrone all the gods, burn all the idols, to make—as Marx said—"out of man, and for man, the supreme being."

The Marxist, being a naturalist and evolutionist, refuses to admit any break in the continuity of development from animal to man. Nothing higher than man exists; no "super-nature" towers above nature. Man represents, at least for the time being, the peak of biological evolution, but there is nothing in him which was not

potentially part of the equipment of his animal ancestor. Though
his work has given him a certain mastery over nature, he himself will
never cease to be wholly and entirely "natural." Out of fear, no
doubt, of making any concessions to *supernaturalism*, I flatly refused
to admit that human psychology contained anything which could
not be reduced to the biological. Even a materialist like Freud, the
founder of psychoanalysis, seemed to us suspect, merely because he
taught the existence of a distinct psychical activity.

In my loyalty to the old Hegelo-Marxist theses, I believed that
man differed from the animal only "in the amplitude of his desires";
with these to spur him, he set himself to work, produce and invent.
His desires grew in proportion to his power to fulfil them, and thus
he moved further and further from his animal origins until the time
came when he denied them outright and fancied himself a kind of
god. But this is an illusion. Man is indeed superior to animals, but
only historically, not ontologically.

From the very outset, man showed himself to be a social being.
Marxists still subscribe to the sociological theory, discarded by sociologists themselves, which holds that primitive man had only a collective consciousness. Individual consciousness emerged gradually
through the dialectical process of the division of labour. Capitalism
represented the apex of individualization. Here, as in all other fields,
Communism, when it finally triumphed over capitalism, would be,
not a step backwards, but a leap forward. It would not destroy
individual, or restore collective, consciousness. Individualism would
be dialectically transcended by a higher form of collective consciousness, containing all the energy and solidarity which the collective
consciousness was thought to possess; but it would also retain all the
conquests of the individual consciousness.

When I said and hoped that Communism would transform man
and create him anew, I was, without knowing it, not far from the
faith of Christians. They too believe in the "new man." This resemblance was once pointed out to me, and I was greatly struck by it.
I soon saw, however, that between the two concepts of man there is
an enormous difference, certainly more fundamental than the ap-

parent analogies. To the Christian, man's renewal must take place within himself, in an interior conversion. I, as a Marxist, was totally unaware of the possibility of any interior, spiritual greatness. During the whole time I was a Party member, I believe I never once heard of St. Francis of Assisi; even if I had heard of him, I should have been quite incapable of understanding him—still more, of admiring him. The one form of greatness that meant anything to me was the Promethean—a greatness directed solely towards social action. I awaited the coming of the New Man as the logical consequence of the transformation of economic conditions.

4 A Professional Revolutionary

UPROOTED

I had always dreamed of going to the university in several different countries. I had no family ties; ever since I was a child I had spoken several languages; there was no particular reason for me to live in one place rather than another. So I entered myself simultaneously at a French Faculty of Letters and a German Faculty of Philosophy, and decided also to attend the lectures of a famous English university. I should thus, I thought, be living to the full the cosmopolitan life which was my birthright.

It was true that in so doing I should stress more than ever the fact that I was rootless, a man without a country. But what did I care! At that time, Communism still went in for being international: it was not until later that it became what Léon Blum called a "Russian nationalist Party." In 1926, then, I had some justification for thinking that by refusing to acknowledge any country, or even any culture, as my own, I was conforming all the more closely to the Communist ideal. When, later on, Maurras' followers called me a *métèque,* I took the insult as a compliment.

As regards my livelihood, I continued to earn it by working as a journalist, as much for German left-wing newspapers as for French. For some years my work consisted mostly of literary and art criticism; then, later on, of reporting international political events.

The kind of life I was now leading cut me off from any chance of making myself useful as a "militant at the base." I really didn't fit into any town or country—just as I hadn't any special social background. The Party, however, never fails to make the best possible use of those who wish to serve it. Its activities are so many and so widespread that it can turn the capacities of any individual to good account. So, by the nature of things and the will of the Party, I found myself becoming, more and more, a kind of commercial traveller of the revolution. My many moves from one town or country to another were no longer undertaken solely for the sake of my studies or my work as a journalist. With increasing frequency as time went on, I was entrusted with various missions by international revolutionary organizations.

To make myself more efficient and more useful in different countries, I learned first Russian and then, as need arose, several other East European languages. I can say from my own experience that anyone who has really mastered three or four languages can learn others almost as a game. The brain seems to acquire a suppleness and adaptive faculty which amazes those who, with only their mother tongue to help them, are making their first stumbling attempt to learn a foreign language. A cosmopolitan, on the other hand, always thinks in the language he is talking. To set against this he runs the risk of never quite making his own the genius of any of the languages he speaks so fluently.

SPIES AND AGITATORS

For seven years I travelled over almost all the countries of Europe, as well as several others. To avoid misunderstanding I had better say at once that my missions had nothing to do with spying for the Soviet Union. The U.S.S.R. no less than any other country—probably more —has its network of spies, and I have no doubt that it is very ably organized. But nothing could be more absurd than to imagine that the Communist Parties in the different capitalist countries were working as conspiratorial organizations for the Russians. The Party militants are too well-known and, almost everywhere, too closely watched by the police to have any chance of making good secret agents. Moreover, the Komintern was well aware that patriotic feeling still ran very high in certain working-class communities, which would have been horrified to learn that Party leaders or militants had handed over the military or technical secrets of their country to a foreign power—even the Soviet Union. Such a disclosure would have seriously impeded Communist penetration into the working masses.

From what I could learn, the spy system was directed by people attached to the various Soviet embassies and protected by diplomatic immunity. It is not *a priori* out of the question that certain Party leaders may at times lend a helping hand to the spies of various countries, if only by putting them in touch with people who will be useful to them. Believing as they do that the true interests of their own country are identical with those of the Soviet Union, they are quite sincere in thinking that by arranging these meetings they are not in any way acting treacherously. But, though the hypothesis may hold good, I must admit that I myself never came across any concrete proof that the Communist leaders of any given country were working for the Soviet intelligence service. And what I think may be taken as absolutely certain is that no well-known Communist personality would ever compromise himself by doing the work of a spy.

During my own "missions" I did, it's true, come across men who, from certain indications, I felt pretty sure were working for the Soviet spy ring. They were always men "of good reputation"—that is to say, they had never had anything to do with the Communist organizations of their own countries, and no one in their immediate circle could ever have suspected them of working for Russia. Among them were many Russian *émigrés* well known for their violently anti-Bolshevik feelings; professional army men of unimpeachable patriotism, officials working in important ministries, and so on. It was not Communist workingmen who handed over to the Soviet secret service the new production methods used in factories, but highly respected engineers, who were far better up in it all.

The spies were not men who had become convinced of the truth of Communism; they were simply men who had been bought Soviet agents kept a very close watch on anyone who could be expected to give useful service. If X lost money on the horses, or Y was known to have an extravagant mistress, the agents would find some way of getting in touch with him and offering him help.

My activities had nothing to do with the work of spies or secret agents. I belonged to the Komintern, or one of its numerous semi-official branches, whereas they were working direct for the Soviet State. It is true that the two institutions were closely allied, and that in the last analysis the success or failure of one had inevitable repercussions on the other. The Komintern, however, laid great stress—even to us militants—on its international character. It would be hard to imagine some counterpart of Thorez in 1930 proclaiming that French Communists would never take up arms against the U.S.S.R., even if it became an aggressor. Moreover, in 1939, after the Molotov-Hitler treaty, the majority of Communists did in fact fight against the allies of the U.S.S.R.

The emissaries of the Party and its branches were not, in principle, supposed to have any relations with the Russian embassies in the countries to which they were sent. Only very important envoys were authorized, at times of serious danger, to take refuge at an embassy. This caution was partly dictated by the wish to keep the U.S.S.R. out of any diplomatic complications. I knew of many cases where Komintern envoys in Poland, Hungary, Italy and other countries where Communism was illegal, escaped to the embassies when the police were on their track; not only were they not given asylum, but they were actually handed over to the police. This, of course, only happened when the embassy in question was certain that the authorities knew where the agitator had taken refuge; when they did not know, he would be coldly asked to leave the embassy by another door.

RED HELP

My first "missions" were in aid of International Red Help, whose work it was to come to the rescue of victims of anti-Communist measures. In every country where there was a minimum of political freedom, the I.R.H. had a great many supporters—not only Communists, but also numbers of men and women who, without being members of the Party, felt its influence either through the Trades

Unions or through various leftist movements they belonged to—not necessarily Communist movements. Many middle-class humanitarians contributed to it, merely because the severity with which Communists were treated in Fascist countries outraged their democratic principles. Taking it all in all, very considerable sums of money were collected—naturally enough, as a high proportion of Soviet citizens were members of the I.R H.

My work was to distribute this money to branches of the I.R.H. in countries where there were Communists in prison. Certain sums were then handed out to the prisoners' relatives and, whenever possible, used to improve their own conditions. The Party was anxious that its members, even behind prison walls, should feel the strength and solidarity of world-Communism. The result, of course, was always to make its militants still more fearless and determined in their fight. Then, too, the I.R.H. came forward to help their dependents whenever the need arose—which meant that the militants themselves were far less likely to dread the dangers of legal action, or the destitution that might befall their families if they themselves were imprisoned or exiled. All this, as one may see, had but a tenuous connection with the humanitarian impulses of the democrats who supported the I.R.H.

My work did not stop at handing over the money collected in the Soviet Union and the democratic countries to the heads of the I.R.H. in countries where there was political repression. I had also to direct and control the working of these organizations, which in such countries were nearly always clandestine, give them the orders of the Central Committee, get the most detailed information I could as to the conditions and morale of the prisoners, and so on.

In Warsaw, Budapest, Sofia and Milan I used often to come across other Communist envoys, also working in secret. Some were busy organizing underground Party cells, others doing work among the young, the trades unions, etc. We were often astounded by the laxity of the police where we were concerned, for we carried out our work almost under their noses; and yet it was very seldom that they managed to catch us.

THE FIRST OF MAY IN WARSAW

I particularly remember the First of May 1929 in Warsaw. Communist and fellow-traveller organizations, all banned in Piłsudski's Poland, had called on the population for a general strike and mass demonstration in the chief square of the capital—the Plac Bankowy. The government, of course, knew all about it, for the call to strike had been sent out in hundreds of thousands of leaflets and announced in the Polish Transmissions over the Kiev broadcasting station. Early on the morning of May 1st the crowds began to pour in by all the large avenues leading to the square—only to find it already swarming with soldiers and mounted and foot police, who broke up the processions with blows of sword or whip. The processions, however, soon reformed, and, waving red flags and singing the "Internationale," set off once more for the square. Once again they were driven off by the guardians of order, and so the game went on for hours, with neither side showing much wish really to come to grips.

We secret envoys were strictly forbidden to take part in revolutionary demonstrations in the countries to which we had been sent. In most "fascist" countries, it is true, the legal penalty for a native who was arrested during a disturbance was no more than a few years' imprisonment. The secret agents of the Komintern, however, ran the risk, if they were caught, of being shot out of hand.

But as it so happened that I was in Warsaw during what promised to be a full-scale demonstration, I wanted at all costs to have as first-hand and lively a report of it for my paper as I could get. So I followed the processions at a short distance—near enough, without seeming actually to be part of them. The sort of ritual game between the demonstrators and the police began to amuse me; I thought it most picturesque and was already thinking what good use I could make of it in my description. There didn't seem to be any real danger, and I saw no further point in keeping my distance from the processions. I was walking side-by-side with a Jewish leftist writer and a very well-dressed young woman. When the processions set out once more for the square, we at last decided to join them: as I wrote earlier, collective enthusiasm is infectious, and we were finding it more and more difficult to be mere spectators. However, to obey Party orders, we retreated onto the pavement whenever the forces of law and order made one of their swoops and put the crowd to flight. This stratagem succeeded several times. Early in the afternoon we noticed that both demonstrators and police were beginning to show signs of weariness and tension. The crowd, no longer content with mere singing and shouting, was getting hold of stones and scraps of iron to throw at the police, who in their turn were losing their previous good nature and hitting out with some force, so that the blood was flowing on all sides. This, as always happens, inflamed the anger and worst instincts of both sides.

Once again, as soon as the crowd dispersed, we went back onto the pavement. But one of the police, either because he had seen what we were up to or because he lost his head, bore down on us and aimed a terrific blow in our direction with the back of his sword. If it had reached me, I should have caught it on my head and it would certainly have finished me. But it hit my companion instead, and he, being much taller than I, took it on the shoulder. It was only the second blow, which had less force behind it, that got me. I don't know how I came to be cut off from my companions, but I suddenly found myself surrounded by the police, while from all sides blows from sword-back (orders had been given that only the flat of the sword was to be used) and whip rained down on my head, shoulders and back. The blood from a head wound blinded me. For the first time in my life, I knew what it felt like to be facing death. I was not in the least afraid. I don't know why, but the situation struck me as very funny, and I roared with laughter. Even if I were not killed on the spot, there seemed little likelihood of my escaping arrest; and as I knew only a few words of Polish the authorities would see pretty quickly that I was a foreign agitator. I knew well enough what that would lead to.

Suddenly there was a general scrimmage, during which I lost sight of the men who were hitting me. I heard a woman's voice speaking to me in a friendly way, but in Polish. I replied in German that I couldn't understand her, fortunately, she spoke German, and told me to follow her quickly. She took my hand and led me swiftly into a house whose door instantly shut behind us. It looked as though her plans for getting me out of my predicament had all been laid.

Halina was a Jewish student. Like almost all Polish Jews, she spoke German fairly fluently. She led me through innumerable courtyards and passages; the pain I felt, especially in my head, was by now so acute that I scarcely knew what was happening. In the back room of a chemist's shop—also kept by Jews—I was given quite an impressive dressing for the cut on my head, and my other wounds were also attended to. Then Halina, who had taken me under her wing in no uncertain manner, went back through other courtyards and passages, as if she had been a courier all her life, and finally brought me to the room which she shared with two friends The three girls put me up and looked after me that night and all the next day, and it was not until the second evening, when everything in the city had quieted down, that this girl who had saved my life accompanied me to a place near my real hide-out. I was not allowed to tell her my address, but this didn't prevent her from finding me two days later The *flair* given by feminine intuition seems to work better than the professional *flair* of the police.

The three students' treatment of me, and the attitude of the chemist and his assistants, first showed me how much sympathy almost all Polish Jews have with Communism. This does not mean, of course, that they were all Communists; many of them, in fact, either because of their social position or their religious beliefs, were strongly opposed to Communism. None the less, any of them would have been ready to run the same risks as my students and the chemist, to hide and help a Communist agitator. It was the natural consequence of the violent anti-Semitism of which the Jews in Poland were victims. They could not fail to take sides with those who opposed the clerico-fascist regime of the time.

On another occasion, when I was at Sosnoviec in Polish Silesia, I went one Sunday, with a party of students and other young intellectuals of the town, for a picnic in the forest. Most of the inhabitants of Sosnoviec were Jews—or, at any rate, all the Communist intellectuals were, and my mission was to them. We were having our picnic on the grass, when we were suddenly set upon by a band of young fanatics, all wearing the badge of some Catholic organization. They beat up men and women with indescribable ferocity; even the children who had come with their parents didn't escape.

This was my first real contact with militant anti-Semitism, and the painful memory of it has never left me. I cannot help thinking of it when I read of the persecutions which Polish Catholics are undergoing. As most of the leading members of the Communist State in Poland are of Jewish descent, one cannot fail to attribute at least some of the sufferings of the Christians to counter-racialism. Certainly, religious or racial persecution is never justified, and I sympathize wholeheartedly with the anguish of my co-religionists in Poland. But I cannot help regretting that they showed themselves quite as intolerant and fanatical when they themselves were in power.

In the 1930's, anti-Semitism in Poland was so violent that even the Communist Party had to come to terms with it. In fact, I was shocked to discover that in almost every town the various para-Communist organizations (Red Help, Revolutionary Intellectuals, Popular Culture and so on) had separate cells or sections for Poles and for Jews. The result is that, even after the setting-up of the Communist regime, the misdeeds of racialism did not cease in Poland. And Moscow, the better to dominate a country which has always been deeply hostile to anything from Russia, skilfully fans the flames of racial hatred within the Communist Party by alternately favouring Polish and Jewish Communists.

THE REVOLUTIONARY INTELLECTUALS

I worked only for a short time as an emissary on behalf of Red Help. In 1929 I became general secretary of an international association of revolutionary intellectuals. Most of the members of the association did not belong to the Party; they were sympathizers, fellow travellers. To begin with, I had a very low opinion of such people, who were quite willing to go part of the way with us—to fight against preparations for war, social oppression and repressive measures on the part of the police—but who refused to submit to Party discipline. At times they even went so far as to criticize the Soviet regime or the strategic *volte-face* of the Party. This, in my eyes, was unforgivable.

As in every left-wing movement whose membership includes both Communists and non-Communists, we Party members held all the key positions. We had orders, however, to do what we could to keep up the democratic appearance of a genuine union of left-wing intellectuals. Within the association was the "Communist section," composed exclusively of Party members. Before every meeting and congress we used to foregather to settle our line of policy and learn the tactical orders issued by those over us in the Party. Whether we ourselves decided to vote for socialist, anarchist or Christian Progressive candidates for the various offices, and whether we supported their program, depended entirely on whether the Party was at that moment favouring intransigeance or co-operation. Yet at the same time we were careful to see that there was always a certain number of non-Communists on the office staff, that the movement might keep its non-partisan façade. We usually elected as president the most famous non-Communist we could get hold of, such as Romain Rolland or Henry Mann. This had the double advantage of making the movement seem non-partisan, and leaving all effective control of it in our hands, for presidents of such eminence were far too busy really to run it. It was the general secretary who assumed authority—and he was always a Communist.

The aim of such associations as ours was to spread Communist influence beyond the sphere of the Party and to induce liberal individualists to act in accordance with Party orders and on behalf of Party interests. We generally succeeded in so handling things that we ourselves were in the majority and met with no serious resistance when we wanted to launch the movement on some campaign which the Party had at heart. Though we sometimes had unpleasant surprises. Quite often, for instance, the liberal, "fellow-traveller" writers and artists were shocked by the methods adopted in Russia by the dictatorship of the proletariat to suppress any opposition, any sign of that liberalism which they themselves held so dear and which had in fact brought them into our ranks. They then proposed, and even at times succeeded in bringing to the vote, motions which, vague though they were (we Communists always saw to it that they were not worded in very precise terms), none the less conveyed some sort of censure of the Soviet Union. The Party was always greatly displeased by these manifestations of objectivity, and it was on us, as leading Party members, that its thunderbolts fell. Yet our orders were to do nothing that could cause a split with the non-Communists. It may be imagined that our work was not always easy.

My direct contacts with Communist working-class cells became less frequent as my functions as "intellectual leader" took on a wider range. From the Communist point of view, the split thus made between the two forms of activity was most unfortunate, and in all probability had some bearing on my future development. With very few exceptions, the only true Communists come from the working classes, and it is only by working in with them very closely that middle-class intellectuals can remain completely "in line." My one means now of keeping in touch with the workers was at the meetings of correspondents of the Communist press who sent in reports on factories and working-class districts. I was, in fact, fairly often deputed to explain to these eyewitnesses the ins-and-outs of the journalist's trade and to teach them to look through Marxist spectacles at the happenings of everyday proletarian life. But I attended these meeting as a teacher—what the workers called a "bonze." I no longer shared with them the humble work of a militant in a Communist cell, as once when I was a member of the Young Communists. I may also have met workingmen among the heads of the Friends of the Soviet Union, for the Party did not want this organization to become a preserve of the middle class. But, as a rule, these were workingmen who had left their original background behind them. Then, too, the Party wanted me to devote myself wholly to work among intellectuals.

However, when I was chosen to be secretary general of the Association, I was only twenty and by no means a great "intellectual" myself. I had published three novels and as many plays, all of them without much literary merit. But my books breathed intense revolutionary enthusiasm, expressed in the most popular clichés of current Soviet slogans. Moreover, I was known to be devoted, heart and soul, to the Cause.

The inaugural meeting of the Association took place in Kharkov. The Soviet intelligentsia was represented in force, and it was through their votes that I was elected instead of the former surrealist A., who had already made his name as a writer. Our Soviet comrades did not seem very well up in the objective situation of intellectual life in capitalist countries—or possibly they thought it of no great importance. There were various features of my temperament which seemed to bring me closer than A. to their idea of an authentic intellectual revolutionary. He never forgave me for the humiliation of which I was the involuntary cause.

The nature of my work brought me into touch with some of the most famous writers and artists of the years between 1930 and 1935. Some were Communists, others had Communist sympathies. To name only those who have since died, I used to meet, fairly regularly, Henri Barbusse, Ludwig Renn, Romain Rolland, Unamuno, Dos Passos, Upton Sinclair, Stephan Zweig. The reader can well imagine that I could not fail to benefit from such meetings.

It was Henri Barbusse who left the most profound mark on this part of my life. He seemed from the very beginning to take quite a liking to me, and often invited me to meals; on several occasions I stayed the night. For years I had been a great admirer of his book, *Le Feu,* and always read his review, *La Clarté.* But the man himself was so much more attractive even than his work! He was the first humanist I had ever met at close quarters. Himself a Party member, he was in a strong enough position to refuse to break off relations with left-wing liberal intellectuals such as Unamuno, Rolland and Henry Mann, during those periods when the Party line hardened. A. carried on an underground war against Barbusse, whom he accused of "lower-middle-class deviationism." When, however, the Komintern resumed its policy of the outstretched hand and the United Front, the Party was grateful to Barbusse for having kept up such useful contacts.

I myself, to begin with, was unpleasantly surprised at the eclecticism that Barbusse showed in his friendships and human relations generally, and the works he admired in art and literature. He never seemed to bother about the political views of the man whose work he was considering. Equally new to me was the concern he showed, in his books and his *Clarté* articles, for subtle shades of meaning. During all my five years in the Party I had been an extremist, contemptuously rejecting any thesis that was in the least conciliatory, or that used any intermediate tones between black and white. It was not until later that I came to see how foreign fanaticism was to my real nature. My extreme intolerance came from my need to brush aside any trace of doubt, to resist any encroachment of weakness. But my own temperament made me more ready than most people to become the disciple of so universalist a mind as Barbusse's.

He was the first person to talk psychology to me, and make me realize how essential it was to see things from the other man's point of view, if I wanted to understand and convince him. The "integrists" of the Party were probably not far out when they accused him of a certain revolutionary romanticism. It was precisely this, however, that gave his talk some quality which affected me far more deeply than the cold objectivity which alone was supposed to have any merits in writings approved by the Party. At one of our Congresses, A. came out as public prosecutor against Barbusse, and even demanded his expulsion for the crime of "middle-class deviationism." I was one of those who stood up most strongly for the great revolutionary writer; I explained how great his influence was over intellectuals throughout the world and made it clear that it was owing to him that many of them had first come to hear of the fight for revolution. Surprising though it may seem, my chief supporters were the Russian members. They themselves would certainly not have admitted him, but clearly they were still under the spell of the old revolutionary romanticism that had characterized all their own great writers, Gorki included.

As for A., the minute he joined the Party he began to show unmistakable signs of being a born inquisitor and counsel for the prosecution. He was a poet of real talent, who had once professed the most extreme individualism, and made no secret of his contempt for Communism and the Soviet Union. No sooner had he decided to join the Party—for reasons I have never been able to fathom—than he became its most biddable member. We never had any liking for each other, and our relations were never closer than was unavoidable between two militants doing more or less the same work. I do not, therefore, know how he squared matters with his conscience—or, indeed, whether he ever consulted it at all. He never showed any embarrassment or the slightest scruple over carrying out the *volte-face* of the Komintern. With astounding self-possession, he would defend a position diametrically opposed to that which, the day before, in front of the same people, he had supported more forcibly than anyone

True enough, I too, like almost all the Party intellectuals, "came into line." But I hardly ever brought myself to do so without first going through a more or less violent inner conflict. And I always felt a slight embarrassment at having to announce publicly that I was in favour of some new position if it was too glaringly at odds with the old To A., even friendship didn't count when it was a question of the general policy—always so disconcertingly fluid—of the Politburo. Before he joined the Party he had been on close terms with most of the poets who were in the fashion round about 1925. He had greatly admired some of them. Now he refused to admit that they had any talent at all. It was not until one of them, Paul Eluard, himself became a Communist under the German occupation, that A. resumed his old friendly terms with him, and once again advertised his genius. But such was his sincerity in bad faith that he did not scruple to write that Eluard did not become a good poet until he joined the Communist Party.

We used often, among ourselves, to talk about "the A. case"—for it was a case, even to us. I know, too, that the political leaders themselves speculated a great deal about him. At the beginning, his excessive anxiety to toe the Party line made them suspicious. But years passed, and neither his loyalty nor his docility was ever at fault. We were forced to admit that we were not up against an *agent provocateur,* but simply a psychopathological phenomenon.

In general, the most subservient and uncompromising of the Communist intellectuals were those without any real talent. Being either self-taught or the throw-outs of good families, they were "intellectuals" only by courtesy of the Party, which was in need of journalists, writers and scholars, and sometimes thought it expedient to confer on some nonentity the name and fame of an intellectual. Some of them were taken in by it, and bore a bitter grudge against the non-Communist press for failing to recognize their genius. Others were more perceptive, and knew that outside the Party they were nothing. Both types were willing tools. In one sense, one may say that these mediocrities had more excuse for their servility than had A

FELLOW TRAVELLERS

Apart from Barbusse's friendship, my meetings with the intellectuals of the Party gave me far less that was of value than my many encounters with fellow travellers. Within the Party itself there were a number of scholars of world-wide reputation, but they towered above me, and I only met them occasionally. Among the writers and philosophers there were few really outstanding minds. But among those who were more or less in sympathy with Communism, and willing to go along with it for quite a considerable way, there were many absolutely first-rate men.

I came in contact with Romain Rolland over the organization of a World Congress Against War, of which he was President. I met Unamuno first at Barbusse's and then later at his own house in Spain. I had occasion to ask Henry Mann and Stephan Zweig to sign some motion or protest. None of these men was a Marxist. They made no secret of their horror at any dictatorship, any restriction of individual freedom by the State. They knew very well that, had they

been living in the U.S.S.R., they would have been wiped out ruthlessly by a regime which they could never have brought themselves
to accept uncritically. But, living as they did in capitalist countries,
these incorrigible liberals almost always backed us up in protesting
against the sins of Fascism in Italy, the Balkans and Poland. They
even protested against any restriction imposed on Communist freedom of action in the democratic countries. They were anti-militarists
and joined us in our campaign against rearmament. To them, this
meant rearmament everywhere. To us, the only crime was the rearmament of the capitalist countries, which we accused of war-
mongering against the U.S.S.R.; Russia's own troops we regarded
simply as the defenders of socialism But we kept this to ourselves.

It was the fashion among Party intellectuals to talk slightingly of
these liberal fellow travellers—though this did not prevent us from
secretly admiring them. We thought it quite natural that they should
protest against violations of political freedom in capitalist and Fascist
countries We never failed to ask them to sign petitions of which we
were the sole authors, or, at least, the instigators; and to attend our
meetings and congresses. But we thought it scandalous that they did
not show complete confidence in everything that bore the rubber
stamp of the Communist Party or the Soviet Union. Their appeal to a
neutral justice seemed to us a fearful anachronism; in our eyes, there
was no common yardstick between the Communist dictatorship in
the U.S S.R. and the Fascist dictatorship in, say, Italy. Was not the
former serving the cause of Truth? Then it was justified; whereas
the latter, the servant of Error, must be treated as something fundamentally evil. We were militants, and therefore partisans, whereas
our fellow travellers claimed to be "above the conflict "

Up to the time of my election as secretary-general of the Association, I knew the liberal intellectuals only through their writings. When
I came actually to meet them I soon changed my mind about them.
Just at first, their neutrality, their Olympian calm, infuriated me.
With a presumption that only my youth and utter inexperience of
human relationships could excuse, I did my best to convince these
men—most of them three times my age—of the necessity of throw-

ing themselves heart and soul into the Communist cause. The kindly disbelief with which they met my arguments seemed to me an insult. But I could not long hold out against their dazzling, their immeasurable superiority. It was impossible not to admire the range and depth of their culture, their knowledge of men and things. Even where Communism was concerned, they had pondered many problems which had never occurred to me at all. Yes, I had everything to learn from them, and nothing to teach them.

My meetings with Barbusse had already convinced me that I had been wrong to let my natural curiosity be put in a strait jacket by the edicts of the Politburo. Through these fellow travellers I came to see the value of what, for years, I had been cutting out of my life, and I made up my mind to broaden my cultural knowledge. Up till then, the one subject I had studied at all deeply was Marxist thought; as regards everything else, I was content with the bare minimum necessary for university examinations. The only contemporary philosophy which I knew at all well was Bergson's. I now let myself be convinced without much difficulty that I should be able to give the Party far more valuable service if I widened the scope of my cultural life. So I began to study all the great leaders of contemporary thought, taking advantage of my wanderings to follow the lectures of Jaspers and Heidegger, Brunschvicg and Lavelle. I no longer walked past works of art with unseeing eyes; whatever town I was in, I always set aside a few hours to visit the museums. My fellow-traveller friends ceased to regard me as a young barbarian, and they and their circle gradually lost their amazement at my having been chosen to play a leading part in a movement of intellectuals.

IN FASCIST ITALY

One of the most interesting missions with which I was entrusted at that time, and one which gave me most, was to Italy. Ever since childhood I had been strongly drawn to that land of light and sunshine, and when I was given orders to go there I was in the seventh heaven of delight. Being a good professional revolutionary I didn't dare to admit that it wasn't only the evils of Fascism that I wanted to see but, as much or more, the beauty of the country and the innumerable works of art strewn all over it. And I had a good excuse for gratifying my curiosity, for I had been told by high authority to behave like a typical tourist, so as to escape the notice of the Italian police.

In Florence, especially, I went far beyond the precautions necessary to hoodwink them. At San Miniato I fell completely under the spell of Fra Angelico. Unfortunately, I did not then know enough about art—Christian art in particular—to get the most out of this first encounter with the Middle Ages and the Renaissance. I had always looked at both periods solely from the point of view of their economic contradictions. The galleries of Florence, and later on the catacombs, pre-Christian ruins, and basilicas of Rome, gave me some idea that there were other aspects, at least as absorbingly interesting as the economic.

The official aim of my visit was to do some reporting for a newspaper which, though it wasn't Communist, was closely connected with the Party. A correspondent's card issued by an openly Communistic periodical, so far from smoothing my path, would at once have brought me under suspicion and made it impossible for me to do my work. The Party had shares in various journalistic enterprises of liberal and bourgeois tendencies, and whenever I was sent on missions abroad I nearly always went, ostensibly, on behalf of these papers.

I travelled right down to Sicily. There, among other places, I saw the famous sulphur mines. The deplorable conditions of the miners, who had to work with almost primitive tools, underground, and with no hygienic arrangements whatever, gave me the material for several pretty scathing articles on the Fascist regime, which claimed to have introduced so many social reforms. I went for walks in the Pontine Marshes, the draining of which had been made so much of by Fascist propaganda; and there I saw how close was the bond between Mussolini's regime and the most die-hard capitalism. The impoverished peasants got little enough out of these reclaimed lands, which simply reverted to the ancient system of latifundia.

My work as a reporter, however, was just a pretext to cover my real activities in Italy. I had been instructed to renew contacts with Italian anti-Fascists, whether Communists, socialists or liberals; and I was given a long list of names, which I copied out in a code to which I alone held the key. If it came to a search, I knew that, whatever happened, the Italian police must never be allowed to find anything that would compromise me or—still worse—endanger the people whom I was hoping to see.

Many of the addresses I had been given went back to pre-Fascist days, and I had to take endless precautions in finding out what had happened to this or that professor, writer, artist, lawyer or doctor. Many of them were living in exile—in Switzerland, America or France. Others were in prison or banished to the Lipari Islands or some remote village in the wildest parts of southern Italy. There were some who had renounced their former ideals and become ardent supporters of the regime. A call I paid in Turin on a certain professor, once well known for his violent opposition to Fascism, nearly cost me dear. He had been strongly recommended to me by one of his old friends, then living in Paris as a refugee. So sure was I that he was completely to be trusted that I was on the point of telling him my real motive in coming to Italy, when I happened to notice the Fascist emblem in his buttonhole. I instantly changed the subject and told him that, quite by chance, I had run into his friend, who suggested that I might call on him and ask him to tell me about the social achievements of Fascism in Turin. Some time later, Communist acquaintances in the town spoke of Professor N. as an unusually whole-hearted Fascist. He would, undoubtedly, have handed me over to the police without a moment's hesitation. Ever since 1946, this charming professor has been one of the most "democratic" deputies of the new republic!

Then I met other men, who had completely severed themselves from public life. Their ideology was still strongly anti-Fascist, but they had given up all hopes of overthrowing the regime, and saw no point in risking their freedom and perhaps their lives by playing at conspirators. In this category there were no Communists. The members of my Party had, of course, been among the most persecuted people in Italy. All intellectuals known to have Communist leanings were either in prison or exile. The fairly important underground movement which the Party had managed to get going in Italy was almost wholly composed of workingmen, amongst whom I had no mandate. Quite recently, however, a few students had joined it, but as they were not on my list, it was by sheer chance that I came across them.

The "old guard" with whom I got into touch in many of the towns usually belonged to the liberal wing of anti-Fascism. There were certainly many Catholics among them, but at that time religious convictions seemed to me quite unimportant I never asked any questions on the subject, and regarded as liberals all anti-Fascists who were not Communists, socialists or anarchists. In the case of most of them, I could present an introduction from friends we had in common. Italians are not suspicious by nature, and when they talked to me they made no secret of their dislike of the regime. Not many of them, however, had any hopes of seeing it overthrown, or were themselves doing anything to overthrow it. They all knew that they were closely watched by the police. Several of them had spent years as political exiles in the Lipari Islands, Apulia or Calabria. As they were known to be under a cloud, they generally found it very hard to earn a living, and in many cases their health had suffered from all that they had gone through. Sometimes they even envied those abroad, who were living the peaceful life of exiles.

They all welcomed me in the most friendly manner, and questioned me eagerly about the U.S.S.R. What perhaps interested them still more, however, was intellectual life in democratic countries, and they were also greatly concerned over the probable outcome of the bitter conflict going on in Germany between Nazism and Communism. As liberals, they had little liking for the Soviet form of government, which seemed far too like Fascism; to them, the touchstone of both systems was that personal freedom in which they were so deficient. My tactful efforts to induce them to join either the Friends of the Soviet Union or the Association of Revolutionary Intellectuals met with small success. They were all middle-aged men, without the fire that one must have if one is to compromise oneself— as they thought and said—"for nothing." But only the anarchists were openly hostile to Communism.

I should have liked to get in touch with the younger anti-Fascists, but when I broached the subject, the "old guard" usually had some very harsh things to say of the rising generation. If one could take their word for it, nearly all the young men at the universities were Fascists, and those who were not were careful to keep out of all political discussions, in which they took not the slightest interest. As always happens under a totalitarian regime, intellectual interests had lost a great deal of their appeal. This was confirmed by my own observation. Almost wherever I went I used to meet young professors and teachers, students and artists. They all welcomed me with true Italian courtesy, but showed little wish to discuss—not only politics, but any subject that was not purely superficial Perhaps, after all, the militant Fascists were the best of the lot; but as they were quite as fervent in their Fascism as I in my Communism, there could be no real dialogue between us. It was only in Florence that I came across something different.

RED FLORENCE

The Tuscan capital is more than the cradle of Italian art: ever since the Middle Ages, it has also been the great centre of thought and political activity. During the Renaissance, it resounded with the thunderous threats of Savonarola's preaching; today, its mayor is that most paradoxical of political Catholics, Giorgio La Pira. In the days of Fascism, Florence, with Milan, was the town in all Italy where resistance to the regime was best organized and most active.

I had an introduction to a certain Professor L., who was well known for his anarcho-syndicalist views. He had spent three years in the Lipari Islands, after which he was allowed to go back to his old home; what was still more surprising, his old chair at the university was restored to him. His views were quite unchanged, but weariness as much as scepticism held him aloof from political life, and he even refused to read the newspapers. He received me very courteously, and asked for news of all the anti-Fascist Italians whom I had met in France, Switzerland and elsewhere. He talked a great deal about his old friend, the philosopher Guglielmo Ferrero, who had taken refuge in Switzerland and was there carrying on a valiant campaign in the world of thought against Fascism. Then he showed me his wonderful library and collection of Old Masters. But I tried in vain to get out of him some information about the regime. He evaded my questions and even, to my great annoyance, showed no interest in the U.S.S.R. There was no doubt about it—this man, whom I found personally so attractive, did not seem to want to help me in my "mission"!

He must have seen how disappointed I was. Suddenly, as we were standing in front of a Florentine Old Master, he asked me whether, instead of wasting my time over an old cynic like himself, I wouldn't rather meet young people of my own age. I saw at once that he wasn't thinking of just any young people, but of those I had been vainly trying to get in touch with. It may be imagined how joyfully I accepted his offer. I was then invited to dinner on the following day.

The next evening, when I went into his drawing-room, I saw a very dark girl of about twenty, small, and very lovely. When she raised her eyes to mine, I saw a look of deep sadness in them. As she is now playing a fairly important part in the political life of her country, I shall only refer to her as "Lucia." Her father, a revolutionary anarchist, had been shot by the Fascists when she was fifteen. The shock was too much for her mother and brought on serious neurasthenia. Lucia had to leave her secondary school and start work in an office; when I met her she was secretary to a big businessman. Her mother had died some months before, and she lived alone in the small family flat. I later took her as the model for the heroine of my novel *Vengeance d'une fille des montagnes*, which I wrote on my return from Italy.

All the time we were his guests, Professor L. saw to it that the conversation was confined to a discussion of literature and art. He did allow himself to criticize, or rather to express deep regret over, the intellectual apathy that had descended on Italy in the last few years; but that was the only reference he made to the regime. He wanted me to tell him about France and Germany, but only from the intellectual point of view; and once again it was brought home to me how one-sided my intellectual development had been. In spite of all my efforts over the last year to widen my outlook, there were still far too many subjects on which my mind was a blank. Lucia, even though her education had been cut short, was a true daughter of Florence, and had extraordinarily good taste, especially in matters of art. But our host was well aware of my impatience to talk to her about other topics than art and literature, and packed us off unceremoniously as soon as dinner was over.

We walked along through the marvellous Florentine night. Lucia told me of her father's struggles and of his death; she spoke of her own life, and her loyalty to the ideals of the father whom she still profoundly admired. She told me that, in and near Florence, there was a fairly large group of young anti-Fascists who met from time to time to read banned books and even talk politics. I gratefully accepted her invitation to meet some of them at her flat on Saturday evening. Even if it did mean that my stay in Florence had to be prolonged beyond the appointed time—well, that couldn't be helped: all the better, in fact! Before we parted, Lucia showed me a way into her flat that I could use without the neighbours' seeing.

At about ten o'clock on Saturday night, seven or eight boys and girls met in Lucia's small dining-room. As far as I remember, there were two girl students, an art student, a schoolmistress and some girls who worked in an office. Several of them were, like Lucia, the children of militant anti-Fascists who had been assassinated or imprisoned. To them, and to several others whom I met through them, the memory of their parents provided an effective antidote to the blandishments of the regime, which always made out that the young were its chief supporters.

The sun had risen when we at last decided to break up the party. A great many cups of very strong coffee had carried us through a whole night of political talk, as impassioned as only the talk of the young can be. Were all the crimes and shortcomings of which they accused the regime to be put down solely to their own youth and legacy of hatred? As I myself was little older or more experienced than they, their way of looking at things just suited me—certainly far better than the oversubtle explanations and scepticism of elderly liberals. That night I felt that I had really pierced to the very heart of Fascism.

I for my part told them at great length what I knew about Soviet Russia. Probably I was no more objective in my praise than they were in their blame. To these young Italians, the Fascist regime was like an enormous extinguisher. They had, as a general rule, no chance of reading any newspapers except those which truckled to the regime, and they did not believe a word of the horrors these newspapers described as perpetrated in Russia by the dictatorship of the proletariat. To them, I was someone who had been there and was speaking of what he'd seen for himself. My accounts tallied at all points with what they had read in the few Communist papers which at that time circulated, in deep secrecy, all over Italy.

They were all sorry that my audience was so small, when they knew so many people to whom the chance of hearing me would have been as great a pleasure and encouragement as it was to them. But I could not postpone the day of my departure any longer, for I had several other towns to visit. But as I thought that this might be my one chance of doing any real organic work among Italian anti-Fascists, it was decided that I should break my journey in Florence on my way back from southern Italy.

On the agreed day, Lucia came to meet my train. Nothing was more likely to throw the ubiquitous Italian police off the scent than to let them suppose that I had come back to Florence to see a pretty girl, so we used the old trick of passing ourselves off as a pair of lovers. Lucia took me to her flat.

On Sunday morning she lent me a bicycle which she had borrowed from some friends, mounted her own, and off we set in the direction of the Apennines, to a place about twenty-five miles outside Florence. After half an hour's ride, we came on two sturdy youths barring the entrance to a ravine who refused to let us through until Lucia had given the password. I could see that there was a bit of play-acting in it all, for they seemed to know my companion perfectly well. Still— either one is a conspirator or one isn't!

We were by no means the first to reach the strip of level ground surrounded by high crags. About twenty young people were already there, and, for nearly an hour, others continued to trickle in When there were about forty of them, I was asked to address them on the U.S.S.R. I therefore described, in detail and as picturesquely as I could, what I had seen and experienced during my various stays there. Then, after a picnic on the grass, they asked me endless questions about whichever aspect of Soviet life interested them most. I do not think I had ever yet come across such interest in the home of Communism—probably because Fascism had misrepresented it more successfully than any other right-wing totalitarian regime. The sun was setting by the time we went down the hill and climbed on our bicycles.

Most of my young audience came from the social level midway between the working class and the professional, which, in Italy, is made up of clerks, teachers and petty officials. But there were a few students among them, and even, I think, two or three genuine workingmen. With the exception of these last, who belonged to a factory cell of the underground Communist Party, none of them was a member of any large anti-Fascist movement. They used to meet in small groups among friends, like the little party I had met at Lucia's. I learnt afterwards that, as a result of my visit, Lucia and a young school teacher joined the Party, and, some years later, they were married. For the time being, it was unanimously resolved, before we left our meeting-place, to found a branch—secret, of course—of the Friends of the Soviet Union. I was proud of my success, which would be scored up on the credit side of my mission to Italy.

That night I took the train that was to carry me from Florence and

Italy. Years later, I discovered another Florence—the Florence of
Savonarola, Michelangelo and Papini. But even this first visit was
enough to give me a deep love for the most beautiful and open-
hearted of all Italian towns. And I felt later that the Florence of
Lucia and the Florence of Papini and La Pira were not really so
very different.

EUROPE OF THE DEMOCRACIES

If I have written at such length about my travels in Fascist countries, it is not because the Party took no interest in left-wing intellectuals living under democratic governments. Indeed, they were my
chief field of activity. This, however, was just the daily round, and I
do not remember much of my many visits to France, Germany, England and elsewhere. Meetings with Communist intellectuals and fellow travellers: lectures on the Soviet Union and sometimes on one or
other of the Fascist countries. . . . Almost wherever I went I
formed relations that were interesting and valuable.

A strange anomaly was rife in the Communist world. In one of
the Nordic countries, the most fanatical revolutionary I met was a
princess of the royal family, who used to speak of her commoner
husband, a highly placed official, as a "frightful bourgeois." She
took in Barbusse's *Clarté* and enjoyed causing a sensation in drawing-
rooms In the capital of a neighbouring country, a group of students
and artists, who gave out that they were Communists, bought between them a small wooden house, had it painted blood-red, and
lived there as a "Communist society." In other words, they pooled
their pay and pocket money, and, most important of all, went in for
free love in a big way and with much ostentation. Most of the ex-
penses of the Red House (as they called it) were met by the spoilt
only daughter of the richest capitalist in the country.

None of this was to be taken very seriously. The Party only chose
to have dealings with royal revolutionaries or eccentrics in so far as
it could make use of them for some immediate purpose. When Soviet
policy was going through one of its "outstretched hand" phases,

such people were useful for getting signatures to protests and appeals. I often wondered what on earth these pseudo-revolutionaries, all of them the children of rich families, would make of the bleak existence, without one ray of romance or fantasy, that prevailed in countries where Communism was in power. There is no room for such revolutionary pranks in the work of socialist construction.

I did not, any more than the Party, attach any importance to these clubs of revolutionaries—or, rather, parlour pinks—patronized by the middle-class young in revolt against their families. In fact, I regarded them with scorn, and condemned them out of hand—though this did not prevent my sometimes feeling very much at home among these young people. Their rambling discussions, their passion for getting themselves talked about, their studied lack of restraint, even their much-advertised immorality, all stood for a kind of release which did me good in the hard, austere militant life that I myself was leading, without either home or country. I entered into their game without any difficulty and quite let myself go over it. But I soon had enough of it and was glad to get back to my dangerous missions in totalitarian countries.

IN THE BALKANS

It was during the school holidays of 1932 that I was given orders to go to the Balkans, which at that time were under a more or less openly Fascist dictatorship which had none of Italy's claims to social awareness.

I first stayed in Prague, the capital of the only country on my itinerary with a democratic government. Then followed Budapest, Bucharest, Sofia, Istambul, Athens and Belgrade. My stay was not, of course, confined to the capitals. I had about a week to spend in each country, and did my best to go to all the important centres, especially those where there was a minimum of intellectual life. But, being a journalist as well as a militant Communist, I didn't fail to take such opportunities as came my way to find out what I could of the political, social and economic problems which pressed so heavily on all these countries.

In the Communist vocabulary, the word "fascist" was used of any regime which refused to give the Party a free hand to carry out its activities, or subjected it to "anti-democratic" pinpricks. Yet we ourselves had no admiration whatever for the famous democratic principles defined by the doctrinaires of the French Revolution. We found it quite right and proper that the Soviet government in Russia should have suppressed all political freedom, not only of the counter-revolutionary parties, but of the *mencheviks* (social democrats) and social revolutionaries (who were more or less anarchists). On the other hand we regarded it as a crying injustice that in Hungary and the Balkans the Communists should be unable to stand for election under their own name. For we made no profession of relativism or eclecticism. As we saw it, all truth and justice were on the Communist side, and any restriction of Communist freedom of action was therefore a kind of sacrilege. "Error" obviously could not claim the same rights as truth. So it was matter for congratulation that error was not tolerated in the country where truth had conquered—the Soviet Union.

If I had been able to see things with a grain of objectivity I should have had to admit that, in most of the countries on my itinerary, the "fascism" in power was nothing very terrible, even from our very partisan point of view. It is true that from time to time Communists were imprisoned, but even on such occasions the government generally felt called upon to use the pretext of some rising or attempted *putsch*—for which in most cases it was not the Communists who were responsible but the wretched peasants. In Bulgaria, for instance, not long before my arrival there, some poor peasant women had killed a rich landowner and set fire to his house. Everyone knew why they had done it; the harvest had been bad, but the landlord had none the less demanded his due. The government used the situation, however, as it always did in such cases, to make a scapegoat of the Communist Party and imprison all its leaders.

Under such titles as the "Workers' Party," the Communists were able, almost everywhere, to stand for election and have their representatives at legislative assemblies. By using the same sort of expedient, they even managed to publish newspapers. No one was taken in by the trick, the "fascist" government least of all. The sociological structure of these countries was feudal, but their leaders had been to the university in France or Germany. They paid lip service to liberalism, and were anxious to be regarded as true democrats in London and Paris. They had been unable to introduce the social, and above all agricultural, reforms indispensable for peaceful social relations. The alarming proximity of the Soviet Union obliged them to ban Communism, but they did not dare to track it down to all its lairs.

Unlike what I had seen of the situation in Italy, in these Balkan countries many intellectuals openly opposed the government and did not attempt to hide their Communist leanings. This was certainly more noticeable in Bulgaria than in Hungary, but nowhere did I have to cover my traces or take the endless precautions that had been necessary in Italy when I wanted to get in touch with opponents of the regime. The chief reason for the difference between the authoritarian governments of Italy and of the Balkans was no doubt the fact that Mussolini's Fascism had a popular origin, and that his dictatorship never ceased to boast a pseudo-progressive and pseudo-revolutionary idealism. Italian Fascism could therefore count on the selfless devotion and impassioned fanaticism of a part of the population, especially the young. In Hungary and the other Balkan countries this was far from being the case. There the dictatorship, more or less heavily disguised as local conditions required, was frankly reactionary, concerned only with protecting a small minority of the privileged class against the claims of the impoverished masses of workers and peasants. This meant that the authoritarian regime was kept in power only by the police, and could make no appeal to idealism. It was not so very unlike what I knew of Tsarist rule.

My first contact with Communist, or para-Communist, intellectual organizations was made in Budapest. These organizations had little of the clandestine about them, except that most of them had been founded without authorization from the government; those which had such authorization were merely told not to use the actual word "Communist" in their official title. The meetings took place publicly, in places known to everyone, and nobody was afraid to voice the most outspoken criticism of Admiral Horthy's dictatorial rule, or express admiration of the Soviet Union. There was almost as little reticence over all this as there would have been in London or Brussels. Our organization of revolutionary intellectuals had a very active branch in Budapest, to which well-known writers, artists and university figures belonged.

I have already said that I happened to arrive in Bulgaria a few days after a disturbance by the peasants, which was used as a pretext to imprison a good many militant revolutionaries. This made it harder for me to make my contacts there than in the other Balkan countries. For some time, however, I had been corresponding with a young left-wing writer and a village schoolmistress who went in for writing poetry. Through them I succeeded in meeting many intellectuals, not Communists, but sufficiently hostile to the regime to consent to join us in united action. Moreover, I discovered that Bulgaria was the one country in Eastern or Central Europe where Russia had great prestige and was regarded with warm feelings by most of the population. This went right back to the days when the Russians had helped the Bulgarians to shake off the Turkish yoke. In every other country, the liberals and even the working people distrusted everything that bore the Russian hallmark, and Communist envoys had to do all they could to persuade them that there was nothing specifically Russian about Communism. We even used to promise them that when the revolution triumphed in other countries, the leadership of the Komintern would soon pass into non-Russian hands. These tactics were especially useful in Poland and Rumania, whose educated classes always looked westwards and regarded the Russians as barbarians. To win them over, we had to say that the capital of the future Communist federation of the world would certainly be Paris. In Bulgaria it was unnecessary to distinguish between Communism and Russia, and it was even politic to emphasize the specifically Slav elements of Communism.

As I have already said was the case in Poland, so too in Rumania almost all the Communist or para-Communist intellectuals were Jews. Rumania had liberal traditions of fairly long standing, and many of her intellectuals had had a French education. They were very conscious, however, of the dangerous proximity of Russia, and for this reason favoured social democracy of the Léon Blum or Mac-Donald type rather than Communism. But as they liked expressing their admiration of such Communist writers as Barbusse and Anatole France, I was able not only to have interesting discussions with them but also to get them to collaborate with us in mixed revolutionary organizations (in which, however, we ourselves kept a firm hand on the reins).

During my week in Greece, I was far more interested in discovering traces of the past than in studying the revolutionary situation of the present. The wonders of Hellenic civilization had always fascinated me, and I identified with deep emotion the places where the great men of antiquity had lived or of which they wrote. We did, of course, discuss various contemporary problems—the U.S.S R., the fight against Fascism, poverty, and so on. But my chief interest lay in comparing the young people I saw with the disciples of Plato and Socrates, and I took a childish delight in any likeness I could detect between the Greeks of today and the Greeks of the golden age.

MY PRISONS

A "professional revolutionary"—Lenin's term to describe someone whose life is wholly dedicated to Communism—must be prepared to see the inside of a prison. It was almost miraculous that I had been able to travel so much in totalitarian countries without being imprisoned myself. On my third or fourth visit to Italy the Italian militia did, it is true, force me to leave the train, and kept me all night at their headquarters (probably while awaiting instructions from higher authority), but all they did next day was to escort me to the frontier and tell me that I was never to set foot in Italy again. It was in Germany that I first knew what it was to be a political prisoner.

From 1931 onwards, the conflict in Germany between Nazis and Communists had assumed the character of a civil war. Almost every day, commando parties carried out armed raids on their opponents' headquarters. Neither we nor our adversaries ever went out except in armed bands. Street skirmishes broke out whenever these hostile groups met, and they often ended fatally.

In the winter of 1931–2, National Socialism won its first great victory at the elections and succeeded in taking over control in several large towns and some *Laender* parliaments. The Communists continued, as before, to carry out their activities openly. They knew very well, however, that they were now barely tolerated, and that even such toleration as they still enjoyed might vanish overnight. They had, therefore, no time to lose in forming organizations which could be adapted to underground fighting. Many people who had come into the Party through sheer opportunism, because they thought it on the verge of victory, now began to desert its ranks. The Nazis organized meetings and conferences everywhere, especially for the young. The speakers were nearly always former Communists, who painted the blackest possible picture of the U.S.S.R., which many of them had visited as Party delegates. The National Socialists, although they called themselves the Workers' Party, had so far found support only among the bourgeoisie and above all the middle class, which had been ruined by inflation and the crisis. But these former Communists swept hundreds of thousands of traditionally Marxist workingmen into the Nazi movement This made our own activities more difficult and perilous, for many of these neo-Nazis were well up in the secrets of our organization and knew that some of our lecturers and agitators went under assumed names.

The first time I was arrested was in May 1932, in a charming little town in Saxony, where I had been giving a lecture contrasting the U.S.S.R. with the Fascist countries I had visited. The police had been told that I was a foreigner—and indeed my accent gave me away. They were given orders to stop me from finishing my lecture tour in Saxony. The National Socialists were not yet in power there, and the liberal traditions of the Weimar Republic did not allow any interference with freedom of thought. I was not sentenced, therefore, but simply held, pending enquiries, for a fortnight—in other words, up to the day of the last lecture I was to give in Saxony.

This brief stay in prison was not in itself at all unpleasant. I had read long ago, with deep feeling, *I miei priggioni,* by the Italian writer Silvio Pellico, who had also been imprisoned for his political activities. I tried in vain to share the romantic and nostalgic longings of this famous victim of Austrian severity towards the Italian nationalist movement. The head warder treated me most considerately. A prisoner sentenced under common law was detailed to wait on me, and the Communists of the town saw to it that I did not have to put up with prison fare. The warder even winked at my being visited by a woman Party envoy who made out that we were engaged. My only worry was that my lecture tour had been stopped and that I could not give my course (for the last year I had ceased to be a student and become a professor). To set against this, I was able, for the first time for years, to have a fortnight's real holiday. I spent all my time reading and writing, and enjoyed the relaxation of at last having a little peace. When I left the prison it was not without a certain regret.

In the autumn of the same year I was again imprisoned; this time there were none of the comforts and amenities that I had had in May. The arrest took place in Thuringia, a *Land* which had been under Nazi control for some months. I had gone there to give a lecture for the Friends of the Soviet Union. The police officer deputed to keep an eye on the meeting took advantage of a row started by a group of Nazis, and arrested me: on this occasion I spent nearly six weeks in prison. I was not actually ill-treated, for until they had the whole of Germany in their hands the Nazis made some show of being democratic. All the same, the privileges that had once been granted to political prisoners had gone by the board. I had to make do with prison food, clean out my cell—and needless to say there was no question of any "fiancée" coming to see me. All books of Marxist tendencies were forbidden. Fortunately, there was nothing to stop me from sending for any other books I liked. Except for the hours I set aside every day to improve my Russian, the long prison days were given up to contemporary literature—German, French and English. Up to that time I had had no chance of getting to know any books but the classics, which were in my scholastic curriculum, and the works of revolutionary authors. I was so busy that even if I had wanted to I should not have had time to hold conversations, *à la* Silvio Pellico, with the birds which used to come and perch on the bars of my cell. On this occasion, as on the former, I did not find my prison existence irksome: it was a useful break in a far too tumultuous life I had time to think and to draw up a balance sheet of the many years I had spent in feverish activity and rushed study. For the first time since I joined the Young Communists, I could go in for a little introspection.

The Nazi Minister of the Interior of Thuringia sentenced me to be expelled from the *Land*. I was accordingly escorted by three S.A. men to the Czechoslovakian frontier and made to leave German territory. A few hours later I was back again. As my expulsion only held good for Thuringia, there was nothing to stop me from continuing my work in other parts of Germany.

SENTENCED TO DEATH

Events in Germany were gaining momentum. On January 29th 1933, Hindenburg summoned Hitler to be head of the Reich government. The banning of the Communist Party was one of the first important steps taken by the new regime. A month later, through the machinations of Goering, the Reichstag was burnt down—an event which enabled Hitler to discard the last pretences of democracy. An outline of the general course of political events does not come within the scope of this book. In so far as I was concerned, they led first to my losing my professorial post, and then to my expulsion from German territory. As I was given orders to return secretly, it wasn't long before I was again arrested. With no respect for juridical procedure, the government informed me that I had been sentenced to death for "subversive activities."

I was imprisoned in the fortress of K , not far from the Czechoslovakian frontier. Here I spent several weeks awaiting execution,
the date of which had been announced to me, with an added touch
of sadism, at the same time as my death sentence. There was, of
course, no question of my having any of the traditional privileges of
political prisoners. The treatment I was given was probably even
more inhuman than that shown to men under sentence of death for
really horrible crimes. What I found hardest to bear, at least to begin
with, was the light that was kept on all night before the grill of my
cell, which prevented my having any sleep before dawn. As I was forbidden to lie down during the day, lack of sleep gradually reduced
me to a state of stupefaction.

It would not be true to say that those days spent awaiting execution left any deep mark on me; they made less impression than must
ordinarily be the case. I was too young and strong to be really afraid
of death For the first fortnight, too, I felt almost certain that my
friends would discover where I was and find some way of getting me
out. As I was merely an unknown writer, I had escaped the terrible
death camps to which the heads of the Party had been sent The
fortress of K. was an old prison for political offenders, and all that the
new government had done was to make the treatment there more
severe than it had been. Many of my Communist friends had inside
knowledge of the place, as they themselves had been imprisoned
there; I thought they'd be sure to think out some way of planning my
escape. I was not, fortunately, forbidden to use the prison library, and
here, as in my former prisons, I used to spend the whole day reading.

Days and weeks went by, and still nothing happened.

I was beginning to wonder if the escape network which the Party
had organized before it was banned was less efficient than we had
hoped it would be—whether, after all, I shouldn't have to make up
my mind to face the traditional twelve bullets. I found it very difficult to imagine my approaching death. From the rational point of
view, I saw it as the final end of an existence which had been short,
certainly, but filled to the brim with intensive life. Yet it was hard—
in fact, impossible—to believe that it would serve no purpose; that

everything in it would return to nothingness An inner voice, not very orthodox from the Marxist point of view, kept whispering that even my death would serve the Cause for which I had lived; that the blood I was about to shed would, in some way, bring forth a harvest *How* such results were to come about, there was nothing in Marxist dialectic to explain. But a man under sentence of death may surely be allowed a few little dialectical heresies.

Forty-eight hours before the date fixed for my execution, when I had given up all hope, the door of my prison opened during the night. At about the time when I should have stood facing the firing squad, I was in Moscow. How could I feel any regrets over such a surprise?

5 *Disillusionment*

Ought I here to describe all that I saw in the Soviet Union during this stay—the longest of any I had made, and which I intended to be for life? What could I add to the accounts written by so many people, both friends and enemies of Communism? Besides, on this occasion, I no longer felt that the U.S.S.R. was something to be discovered; I thought I knew it very well. I had already been there several times. Almost without noticing it, I had been present at the successive stages of the extremely inconsistent Stalinist policy. I now knew enough Russian to be able to talk to people without difficulty, and even to give lectures and make speeches. There was nothing to stop me from fitting perfectly into the Soviet background, and I fully intended to do so.

As I do not want this chapter to swell to the proportions of a large tome, I must keep to the main object of this book and write of people and things only in so far as they had some direct bearing on the development of my life. Some people will no doubt be surprised that Soviet Russia disillusioned me, not in 1925, when I first went there, but ten years later. In spite of the hardships of enforced collectivization from 1929 onwards, the poverty in 1934-5 was undoubtedly less than on any former visit. But on those earlier occasions—how long ago they seemed!—there was also more hope; it was that which had made it possible to see some meaning in even the worst sufferings.

THE COUNTRY IS NOT THE SAME

As soon as I was in Moscow, I asked permission to settle for good in the Soviet Union and there work to the best of my ability at the task of socialist construction. Before long I was nominated as Professor of Philosophy at Tiflis University. I was overjoyed, for the inhabitants of Moscow all went about with such anxious expressions that I had no wish to live there myself. Besides, the Caucasus was a new world for me to discover.

Before taking up my new post, I had to make a rapid three-months' tour of European Russia. I revisited the Ukraine, the Crimea, Leningrad and the Kuban Republic; I even went as far as the Urals. If I had to find one word to sum up the impressions left on me by this far-flung lecture tour, I should say that the whole of the U.S.S.R. seemed to me one vast workshop. In places where, a few months earlier, I had seen small villages, there were now industrial towns of over 100,000 inhabitants apiece. In the Urals I saw the mushroom growth of an immense industrial enterprise (*kombinazi*), where before there had been absolutely nothing. Even the steppes of the Ukraine and the Kuban Republic were no longer what they had been from time immemorial. They were covered with *sovkhoses* (State farms), stretching for tens of thousands of hectares. Equipped with the most up-to-date machinery imported from America or Germany—or perhaps already made in the huge Soviet factories which were so organized that in next to no time they could turn out tanks instead of tractors—these *sovkhoses* were planned to produce quantities of all the foodstuffs which the towns and industrial centres were going increasingly to need, and which traditional peasant agriculture would never have been able to supply.

I learnt, of course, that the Five Year Plans (this was the second) had imposed so rapid a tempo on industrial and agricultural collectivization that it had led to quite a few disasters. There were, it is true, cases of sabotage from time to time, but the chief cause of the trouble was excessive enthusiasm. "Socialist emulation" started in the offices of the central administration, which did not always stop to think what was in fact possible, and demanded the impossible. It was made a point of honour to carry out the Five Year Plan in four, or even three years, and this was seldom done without detriment to quality. Moreover, when some enterprise had got ahead of the plan in this manner, it would often be unable to function further, for the simple reason that some other enterprise, which was supposed to supply it with raw materials or fuel, had not caught up with it. There have been so many accounts in books and newspapers of the chaos resulting from the first Five Year Plans, that I need not stress the subject. And yet, however much justification there might be for these jokes and criticisms, even someone as unversed in technical matters as myself could not help seeing that the Soviet government was rapidly carrying out the industrialization of the most backward country in Europe. Using whatever means came to hand, it had undertaken an industrial revolution. I knew enough history to remember that even in France and England revolutions of this sort do not take place painlessly. Setbacks and inadequacies in this sphere did nothing to lessen my admiration for the Soviet Union.

THE FAVOURED ONES OF THE REGIME

I was at Odessa, the largest port in the U.S.S.R., on the Black Sea. Catherine the Great had founded it, and its first governors were French; it is still the most Western-looking of all Russian towns. The Communists have not destroyed the enormous statue of the Duc de Richelieu which, architecturally speaking, makes it so like some large French provincial town. It is true that when I saw it, it had little of its former splendour left. The commercial and tourist links between Communist Russia and the outside world are incomparably fewer than they ever were in Tsarist days—though even the Tsars did not always take kindly to the thought of their country's being exposed to new ideas from the West.

The port of Odessa gave me the impression of being almost abandoned and empty. Now that the Balkans have been subjugated by Russia after the second World War, the port may perhaps have regained a little of the life which, as we know from countless travellers' tales, characterized it before the October Revolution.

After the lecture I had come to give, I was invited to a reception. It was in fact a social reception, in imitation of those given in all good middle-class society, and bearing no resemblance to the very free-and-easy gatherings of Comrades that I remembered from earlier years. Only the élite of the town turned up in the fine drawing room of one of the chief leaders of the Party, who lived in what had once been the house of an import merchant.

I saw several members of the higher ranks of the Party and Syndicates, heads of industry, a few writers and artists then in the public eye, some officers, and, inevitably, a certain number of the local heads of the G.P.U. These last were easy to recognize by their arrogant bearing and furtive eyes; they were, in fact, typical of the police in all totalitarian countries. There were women, too, of course —the wives and daughters of these prominent people.

I knew very well what terrible sufferings and privations the Soviet masses were then enduring in the name of socialist construction. To buy the machinery it needed from abroad, the U.S.S.R. was forced to export. Now the only commodity that the capitalist world wanted from Russia was food—of which she herself had not enough to meet the needs of the population. Moreover, intensive industrialization had drained the countryside of much of its manpower; and agricultural collectivization, in that first stage of adaptation, had had the fatal result of reducing output. The government was therefore compelled to cut still further the meagre rations of the people, who had not known plenty since the revolution of 1917.

It was, then, with a sense of shock that I saw being served, at this social gathering in Odessa, large quantities of caviare, butter, and other food hard to come by in Russia; vodka was flowing freely, and there was plenty of good wine from the Caucasus and Crimea. I knew, of course, from my own experience, that when the five Year Plans first began to impose a rigid discipline and serious restrictions on the people, the government had thought it politic for external propaganda to entertain foreign guests in a very lavish way. But here it was not a question of foreigners. It was the heads of the regime having a blow-out among themselves.

I was, if possible, still more horrified by the conversation of the Soviet bureaucracy of Odessa. Ten years before, the Party militants in the Soviet Union, when they wanted to convince their guests of the strides that socialism had made in Russia, used to boast of all the changes for the better that had been made in the workers' lives. They were especially fond of drawing attention to every sign of equality among the population. When they saw that we were horrified by some spectacle of poverty or want, they never failed to point out that the heads of the government shared the same conditions. Did not all Party members, factory hands and Commissars alike, draw the same pay? It went without saying that the privations were merely temporary, and that when the fruits of progress appeared—as they soon would—there would be equal shares for all.

The situation now was very different. There were probably no real workingmen left among the Party members; those referred to as workingmen in statistics had, no doubt, really been so at one time, but had long since been swallowed up in the bureaucracy. The Party was taking on more and more of the character of a lay order—something like the Templars or Teutonic Knights of the Middle Ages; a forcing-house for the political and technical leaders of the Soviet Union.

At this reception in Odessa of which I was the guest of honour, the imposing boss of some enterprise or other decided that it would be a good idea to show me that socialism in Russia was no longer a distant dream but had become an established fact. He took his pay-sheet out of his wallet, and I could thus see with my own eyes that he and those of his standing were earning from twenty to thirty times as much as an ordinary workingman. A high Party official, who overheard what we were talking about, came up and proudly assured me that he earned even more. With a touch of irony I asked Comrade N., a novelist much in favour with the Politburo, what his salary was. N. was a writer of very little talent, but he had been the first to have the bright idea of writing a novel in praise of collectivization, and this had made him the white-headed boy of the Russian literary world of the 30's. As is often the case with mediocrities, he had no sense of irony, and began at once to tot up, in front of me and several other people, the considerable takings of his trade. The most surprising part of it all was that his hearers, far from blaming him, all seemed to be listening with great respect and perhaps even with secret jealousy.

I was much perturbed by what I'd seen at this reception, and in the days that followed I observed the new "high society," of Odessa and later in other towns, with a more watchful and critical eye. I had little experience of social life, but I could not fail to see how hard the privileged members of the regime were trying to seem like the "upper classes." This was especially so in the case of the women. Not one of them was really well-dressed, but they all put on great airs as they went about flaunting furs—and some of them, jewels—which had been in fashion before the 1914 war They had bought them, no doubt, from ruined members of the once prosperous middle class. Both men and women drank heavily and talked, not only very loudly (a general characteristic of Russians at all times and in all circumstances), but with the conceit typical of upstarts. The women, especially, were arrogant in the way they spoke to servants (for there were servants again in Russia!). Everyone talked contemptuously of workers and peasants; the word "moujik" had taken on its old unfavourable connotations among these leaders of society. The moujiks, they insisted, were lazy, ignorant and boorish—quite incapable of understanding the lofty aims of all the plans for industrialization and collectivization. These gilded few at the top were really shocked by the people's apparent lack of enthusiasm for socialist emulation, and by the grudging spirit in which they accepted the sacrifices laid on them by the "rapid progress of the country towards socialism."

THE SOVIET UNION NO LONGER CLASSLESS

When I was back in my hotel room after this reception in Odessa, I felt, for the first time since I had been a Communist, a sense of uneasiness, which I no longer tried to stifle, over Communism itself. Even the hotel, which was part of the Intourist network, added to my perturbation. It was the former Hôtel d'Angleterre, now reserved solely for foreigners, and those at the head of the Soviet government. Its blatant, vulgar luxury was typical of the newly-rich—as typical as the drawing room where I had spent the evening. We had all been so much more at our ease in the humble inns which housed the foreign delegations during the 1925 celebrations of the October Revolution!

My readers may remember that it was the ideal of equality which, more than anything, had drawn me to Communism. Was it not this ideal which had inspired all social reformers, from Plato to Lenin? The overthrow of capitalism, the abolition of private property—in short, the revolution, with all it stood for—had, for me, the one supreme aim of creating a form of society in which complete equality would prevail. I did not, of course, imagine, any more than other Communists did, that this magnificent ideal could be realized overnight. The injuries inflicted by capitalism were so serious that one would have to accept human inequalities, both mental and physical, as something inevitable for a long time to come. Yet had not Marx and Lenin written that in the future Communist society all men would be, if not geniuses, exactly, at any rate highly gifted? And as, according to our dogmas, the economic system was, in the last analysis, the basis of everything, it seemed perfectly natural to me to attribute all the inequalities of former society to capitalism. And, obviously, as soon as the revolution triumphed, the first result would be that all inequalities would disappear. The utmost concession I was prepared to make was that, during the transition period, it might be necessary to put up with inequalities of pay in favour of non-Communist specialists whose help was needed in the work of socialist construction. This, indeed, was done, even under Lenin. But how could it seem anything but a terrible betrayal that even Party members should feel the lure of personal gain?

When I once expressed my concern over all this to a certain eminent person, he handed me one of Stalin's last speeches, in which the Father of the People condemned egalitarianism outright as a petty-bourgeois utopia. Strangely enough, I had already read the speech, but had paid no great attention to the sentence in question—probably because I could not believe that it meant what it said.

The reception in Odessa had shown me an aspect of the evolution of the Soviet State which I had overlooked. I now sought signs of it everywhere—and found them. One would have had to be blind indeed not to see that, so far from being any nearer to the abolition of class distinctions, Soviet society was again splitting up into classes which were not only distinct, but opposed. I was astounded to see that, in general, the representatives of the ruling class met only each other: they had their clubs, and tended more and more to marry within their own circle. At one time the law saw to it that the sons and daughters of working people formed the majority of the students at the universities and engineering colleges. Now the children of Party leaders made up a steadily increasing proportion of those destined one day to take over the control of the State. True, the law had not altered. What had happened was quite simple: Party and Syndicate officials, officers of the Red Army and Militia, stakhanovites —all had been officially labelled "workers." Statistics could therefore continue to emphasize the working-class character of the intelligentsia.

After the revolution, almost all the houses of the middle classes and aristocracy were occupied by working people, who in many cases burnt the parquet floors and ruthlessly destroyed the statues and pictures. The great reception rooms were divided, by wooden or brick partitions, into flats, all of which looked like slum tenements. Now that the principle of equality had been rejected as heretical, the working-class families—whenever it was still worth anyone's while to do so—were turned out of these houses to which they had not been born. In Moscow, Leningrad, Kiev, Odessa I was by turns the guest of a Party leader, an official writer, a general, the director of a factory— all of them living with their families in magnificent private houses or even in the former palaces of Grand Dukes. Though they were clearly not quite at their ease in these new surroundings, they did their best to ape the glories of days gone by.

In the Crimea and the Caucasus, by the sea and in the mountains, the old palaces of the aristocracy and the great capitalists had at first been turned into rest homes for working-people or holiday homes for their children. From 1930 onwards, these palaces, one after another, were taken away from the workers. Only those who had distinguished themselves in some quite outstanding manner by their work for the Party, still, in 1934, had the privilege of going there for convalescence or holidays. The finest of these palaces were reserved for officers, prominent technicians, or Party bureaucrats. And I remembered the sceptical shrugs of my working-class companions at N. and L., when we young Party intellectuals used to air our plans for the bourgeois villas and private houses, which were all to be handed over to workers and ragpickers.

THE END OF A DREAM

My Communist susceptibilities had been severely shaken by the spectacle of a State, governed by men of my Party, which in so short a time had again split up into mutually opposed classes. I was surprised that I had not noticed it before, for, as I told myself, so serious a betrayal could not have taken place overnight. But my Communist faith had prevented my seeing people and things as they really were—or else I had not paid much attention to what I did see. Everything now had taken on a new significance. I could no longer shut my eyes to the fact that for the last ten years developments in the Soviet Union had been moving, not in the direction of equality, but towards a steadily increasing accentuation of inequality, between various social categories. It was useless for official propaganda to try to brush aside the evidence by continuing to assert that it was the proletarians who got most out of the regime, when this merely meant that those who got most out of the regime had originally come from a proletarian background.

If there had even been harmony between the different social classes and categories! But one glance was enough to show that there was not only difference but opposition. I even saw unmistakable signs that a new class war was beginning. Whenever I had occasion to talk to workingmen, I could see that they made no secret of their hatred and contempt for the new privileged class. While I was staying in the Donetz Basin, an overzealous stakhanovite had just been beaten up by workers whose norm of work had been raised. Elsewhere, the secretary of a sovkhose was killed by the peasants. The government's reply to all these acts of despair was to send punitive expeditions, which carried out savage reprisals. I began to think that fundamentally a working-class district in 1934, in the Soviet Union, was not so very unlike what Gorki had described in *Mother*. With this difference, however, that there was now no hope for the victims of oppression.

In 1917, the first act of the Russian soldiers who had rallied to the Revolution was to tear off the epaulettes and decorations of their officers. An Army commissar, ranking above the military commander, was introduced into every unit. Seventeen years later, the Red Army again had its generals and marshals, all wearing epaulettes even more encrusted with gold than they had been in Tsarist days, and with still more dazzling galaxies of decorations on their chests. In fact, Stalin was soon to confer on himself the title of Marshal. Even civilians were thought to need the stimulus of medals and ribbons, and the "Orders" of Lenin, the Red Star, and so forth, were created. How far away—quite forgotten—were the days when the Communist government of Russia proclaimed its love for equality and simplicity!

Anyone who knows the importance which militant Communists attach to the egalitarian ideal will understand that as soon as I realized how completely this ideal had been jettisoned, no further "betrayals" by the Soviet leaders could ever come as a surprise to me. On one occasion I was in the Kuban Republic with a team of "activists" who had been sent to spur on collectivization. The moujiks were, indeed, somewhat tepid in carrying out the Party's wishes that they should form a kolkhoz, and, when forced to do so, put so little heart into working land which no longer belonged to them that there were serious doubts as to whether the production norms fixed by authority would ever be achieved. So we saw them working under the watchful

eye of militiamen armed with large revolvers and knouts. Any slow-
ing down of the stakhanovite working-rhythm was punished with
repeated blows of revolver butt or knout. The most stubborn of these
Cossacks—a race always famous for its love of freedom and independence—were arrested, sentenced (out of hand, and without any
judicial procedure) to years of forced labour, and packed off to
Siberia, Turkestan or the Ural mines.

THE UGLY FACE OF DICTATORSHIP

Despite the fear which prevented any mention of these matters
above a whisper, I learnt without much difficulty from the villagers
themselves (but also from the activists and militia) the means that
had been taken to induce the peasants to accept the kolkhozes.
Every night, militiamen used to break into the farms and ransack
them, tearing off the floor boards and rafters, and ruthlessly confiscat-
ing grain, meat and domestic animals. The harvest had been bad that
year in the Kuban Republic. None of the villages I visited had been
able to hand over the amounts of grain and meat which the government demanded. The government, however, made it a point of honour to outstrip its own plans, and sent off teams to the villages to
seize everything which the moujiks had been able to set aside for
their own needs. The result was that in every town and village one
saw hoards of starving peasants begging for a crust of bread or a
potato. Yet did not the Russian Communist Party, at Lenin's express
wish, call itself the Party of Workers and Peasants?

The year 1934 was not the first when I had seen extreme poverty
and forced labour in the Soviet Union. Up till then, however, I had
believed that they were mere growing pains, and that soon there
would be unrestricted freedom and prosperity for all alike. But now
famine, the coercion made necessary by agricultural collectivization,
forced labour—all seemed to me horribly sinister, for nothing now
gave one any encouragement to hope that freedom and well-being lay
ahead for the whole population. The higher ranks of the government

appeared completely deluded and satisfied; they had no sense of solidarity with the hapless masses. Socialism had ceased to be the dream of their hearts. They themselves were doing very well out of the privileges which the government conferred on anyone with the least scrap of power; they firmly believed, therefore, that socialism had already been achieved, and looked no further. We had always justified the dictatorship of the proletariat as a historical necessity during the transition period, until the class divisions were finally abolished; the moment it was announced that socialism—a classless society—was already in existence, the dictatorship of the proletariat became a horrible farce.

At one time, I had been pleasantly surprised by the extraordinary zest of the Russian people—their capacity for enthusiasm, their bubbling gaiety, their unquenchable hopefulness. Now, look where I might, I saw dull eyes, utter apathy, fear. The only light that would sometimes flash for a second in the eyes of some peasant or working-man was a gleam of hatred.

For years I had honestly believed, and proclaimed my belief to others, that the terrible political police of the Soviet Union (known successively as the Cheka, the G.P.U., the N.K.W.D. and now the N.W.D.) did its gruesome work only among the enemies of the revolution—who were thus the enemies of the toiling masses. Being a Marxist, I professed utter contempt for all sentimentality, and felt no pity for people who were supposed to be sabotaging socialist construction. Now, after what I'd seen in Odessa, the Kuban Republic and elsewhere, how could I go on identifying the regime with the Russian people? It was perfectly obvious that the regime sent out its militia, not against the enemies of the people, but against the people themselves. The so-called kulaks, whom official propaganda made out to be exploiting the people, were really, as I soon saw, just small farmers, who were deported merely because they headed the resistance to collectivization. Besides, every transport that set out for the distant labour camps contained large contingents of workers from the mines and factories. So little was needed, in those days, for any man to be accused of sabotage!

THE CHARM OF GEORGIA

Towards the end of June I at last reached Tiflis, which, geographically speaking at least, is no longer part of Russia. I know that even in Russia itself the scenery is not quite so monotonous as my memory makes out. The alternation, according to the region, of steppes and impenetrable forest, with huge rivers flowing through both, usually so slowly that they do not seem to be moving at all, has left me with a crushing sense of immobility, and quite wiped out all mental pictures of the sunny hillsides and rolling country which, none the less, I often saw and admired.

In Georgia the scenery is entirely different from what one thinks of as Russian. I had a pleasant feeling of having stepped into another world. The towering peaks of the Caucasus, the fruit trees and flowers, all reminded me of the Mediterranean countries; the hot sun and intensely blue sky made me feel as if I were in the Maritime Alps. Yet it was not quite the same. The Caucasus Mountains had something frightening about them—something monstrously large. If at that time I had known the Atlas Mountains in Morocco, it is of them that the Caucasus would have reminded me, rather than the Alps of Provence.

The people of Georgia seemed to me as unlike Russians as the countryside was unlike Russia. I had always felt very much drawn to the Russians. Their spontaneous generosity and outgoing natures had captivated me from the first. Yet I had never been quite able to fit in with them. Like other races, they have been influenced by the land they live in. Now I soon tire of steppes and forests, and find that they become a bit boring. If I am with Russians for any length of time, I have exactly the same feeling. Their habit of talking for hours on end, their passivity, their lack of any critical faculty as we in the post-Cartesian West understand it, their nostalgic melancholy, always give me a sense of oppression. The harsh discipline imposed for the sake of the Five Year Plans, prolonged privations, and the dread which the G.P.U. had driven deep into their souls, seemed, moreover, to have half-crushed all that was best in the Russian character. The exuberance was now artificial, they no longer dared to be spontaneous, and even their discussions lacked the fantasy which at one time had made them bearable.

In Georgia I met a completely different people. Even in the most civilized and cultured of them, it was not hard to see the characteristics of a tough, hotheaded mountain race. For years they had fought Russia for their independence, and were far from resigned to her yoke, even now. The fact that Russia herself was under the heel of their compatriot, Zozo Djugasvili, alias Stalin, seemed to them a piece of poetic justice: it may even have made the rigours of the regime a little easier to bear.

Probably in the higher valleys the clutches of Moscow had some difficulty in taking hold, and one could be more or less wholly unaware of the changes that had come about.

Georgians are gay, energetic and little given to passive resignation. The women are very beautiful; I do not think I have ever been in a country whose women, taken as a whole, are so attractive.

I soon saw that Georgia, even if it were not Russia, was none the less an integral part of the Soviet Union. As in every other part of its vast territory, colossal statues of Lenin and Stalin "adorned" the main squares in Tiflis, Gori and all the other towns. Everywhere, too, the G.P.U. militia was undisguisedly present. The orders for collectivization, for exceeding the norms laid down in the Five Year Plan, were exactly the same here as in Leningrad or Kharkov.

In all probability my impressions in the Caucasus region would have been different if, when I came to Tiflis, I had not already had the shock of meeting people who had feathered their own nests under the regime. Certainly the reason I was at first so delighted at finding Georgia so different from Russia was that my unconscious hoped to shake off the crushing sense that the revolution had been betrayed. It was a disappointment to find so many Russians in Tiflis: the sight of them made me afraid that I might see a repetition of what, for the last few months, had been causing me such acute distress. There was, of course, a good deal of injustice towards the Russians in these complex feelings. I had no reason to think that the most pitiless torturers of the G P.U. in the Caucasus were Russians rather than Georgians. Indeed, even in Moscow and other large towns in Russia proper, I had met several of the cruellest members of the Cheka, who *were* Georgians. And Stalin himself, whom more and more I was coming to look on as the arch-traitor of the revolution—was not he a Georgian?

But instinctive reactions seldom have much regard for objective justice. It remains true to say that the many Russians I saw in Tiflis, and the almost aesthetic distaste I felt at the sight of them, counted for much in the judgment I was to make of yet another *volte-face* on the part of the Kremlin.

STALIN DISOWNS THE INTERNATIONAL

Internationalism is, and always has been, one of the motive forces of almost every communist or socialist theory. Until the 1930's, Marxists, too, regarded it as one of the principal articles in their creed. How feelingly, and with what conviction, used my companions and I to repeat Marx's famous slogan in the *Communist Manifesto:* "Proletarians have no country!" The same *Manifesto* had flung its battle cry to the world: "Proletarians of the world, unite!" Thousands and thousands of times I had heard revolutionaries of every country and tongue shout together: "Proletarians of the world, unite!" Indeed, the phrase had long been the rallying-cry of all Marxist revolutionaries.

From the earliest days of the working-class movement, the abolition of nationalism had been held up as the first condition for establishing the reign of universal brotherhood. Up to 1933 a great many Communists in every country used to learn Esperanto. We believed that only an artificial language, a language which did not really belong to any nation, could serve as a means of communication between men of all races. This would remove the risk that any one country might come to dominate others by the spread of its own language and culture. In the early stages, Esperanto was to be each man's second language, taught in every school alongside his mother tongue. But we greatly hoped that, later on, when several countries were enjoying the benefits of Communist rule, Esperanto would gradually take the place of national languages. Judged by the great principle of historical materialism, a number of separate nations, each with its own language and culture, seemed to us quite as anachronistic as the small craftsman, or private property. I already knew several families in which the husband and wife, being of different nationalities, used Esperanto as their first language—the language they spoke all the time to one another and to the children. And the children, who learnt an international language before they knew their own, seemed to me the pioneers of future society.

Up to 1929, Communist Esperantists belonged to the world-wide organization known as S.A.T. (*Sennacia Associo Tutmondo*), which included socialists, anarchists, syndicalists and others. The Soviet government strongly supported the movement. International Congresses were held in the Soviet Union, and Communist Esperantists had no difficulty in getting permission to take part in Congresses held in capitalist countries. But, from the very start of the first Five Year Plan in 1929, Communism began to be increasingly infected by the spirit of intolerance and totalitarianism: in fact, sectarianism became the chief note of what will go down in history as Stalinism. It became almost impossible for Soviet citizens to leave the country. The Komintern even looked askance at Communists in capitalist countries who belonged to any organization which was not under its own strict discipline. We had, therefore, to resign from the S.A.T. and form the International of Proletarian Esperantists (I.P.E.), under the direct control of the Party. But even this was only a respite. From 1933 onwards, Stalin completely disowned internationalism, and the Party thenceforth regarded the Esperantist movement as a heresy. Several of its Russian leaders were shot.

It seems unlikely that Stalin acted out of any theoretical conviction when he broke with the international traditions of Communism and became the champion of Russian patriotism, imperialism and even chauvinism. In fact, it is more than probable that the Father of the Peoples did not even see that he was turning his back on the whole long socialist tradition. He was a very astute strategist, but had no real intellectual gifts at all; the question of any agreement between theory and practice hardly seemed to enter his head. The *theory* that he professed continued to be undiluted Marxist-Leninism; but as far as practice went, he was guided by only one thought—his wish to remain in power. He was in no sense a Cartesian; clarity of thought meant nothing to him. Russian chauvinism, international socialism— he believed he was being equally loyal to both; or at any rate, he believed they could both be equally helpful to *him*, by keeping him in the saddle.

The terror which obsessed him all through his reign was the possibility of outside aggression; and Hitler's rise to power seemed to confirm his fears. Many of the countries bordering on Russia—Poland, Hungary, Rumania, Turkey—had governments of fascist tendencies which made no secret of their hostility to the Soviet Union. To me, the frenzied rhythm of Russian industrialism and collectivization was justified by the wish to put the country on a footing of self-defence against possible aggression. But it led to strong opposition within the country, not only among the peasants but among the factory workers too. Stalin no doubt saw from then onwards that the Communist ideal had not yet sunk deeply enough into the Russian soul to weld all Soviet citizens into one inseparable whole against external attack: it was this realization that made him appeal instead to those patriotic feelings which in Marxist theory are considered extremely reactionary. Seen from this new standpoint, internationalism could not fail to appear as a source of weakness.

This is how I see these matters now that I am able to judge them objectively. But at the time I could not resist a terrible sense of disillusionment. How could I fail to think it a betrayal that Stalin himself, the men round him, and, at their orders, the press, should all sing the praises of Russian greatness in almost lyrical language? For years the Soviet government had boasted of having done away with the Tsarist empire; now, lo and behold, it was claiming this empire as a birthright! Anything that flattered Russian national pride had suddenly become admirable. Writers who had once been looked on as reactionary were again being studied in the schools, and their works were back in all the libraries. When Yasnaïa Poliana was turned into the Tolstoi Museum I was, needless to say, delighted; but I could not help feeling sorry that the cult of Tolstoi was not based on the universal and pacific elements in the author of *War and Peace*. On the contrary; what Soviet youth was expected to admire in him was all that was essentially Russian.

Ivan the Terrible and Peter the Great ceased overnight to figure in history books as oppressors of their people, and turned into the great founders of Russia, whose most illustrious heir, born to carry on their work, Stalin claimed to be. The Soviet newspapers had already begun their idiotic campaign of "proving" that every important invention and discovery owed its existence to Russian genius.

At Tiflis University we professors had, of course, to fall into step with what our predecessors had taught before 1917. To Georgian youth we seemed, as they had done, the ideological agents of Russian imperialism. There was no longer any question, as there had been just after the Revolution, of encouraging the young to love humanity as a whole, or of teaching them the rich culture of their own country. We had to "prove" the all-round superiority of Russia.

To me, however, the chauvinism of the Kremlin was not as bad as the attitude of French, English and other Communists. I used to have copies of the *Daily Worker* and *L'Humanité* sent to me from time to time; there, too, all traces of internationalism had vanished; they were simply Russian newspapers which happened to be printed in English or French. The editors seemed completely shameless about passing on to their readers the absurd lucubrations of time-serving Russian publicists and scholars, who were expected, at every turn, to come across fresh evidence of the towering superiority of Russia over all other peoples of the earth.

TERROR AND DISTRUST

By birth, education and conviction, I was a cosmopolitan; to me the most terrible aspect of the "Stalinite betrayal" concerned the question of internationalism. I should have greatly liked to know

what my companions at Tiflis—both colleagues and students—
thought about it. In both groups I had extremely good friends, with
whom I spent many happy hours, talking, hearing music or rambling
through the glorious valleys of the high Caucasian mountains. I was
shown countless signs of friendship, and had no reason to doubt that
they were genuine.

Yet it was almost impossible for me to learn anything of what my
friends really thought or felt about the innumerable twists and turns
of Kremlin strategy They would speak quite openly on any subject,
as long as it had nothing to do with politics. Over this, there was a
general taboo; everyone knew that the least mention of it ran one into
appalling dangers.

I myself did not dare to confide my doubts or my secret revolt to
anyone. How was I to know that the companion with whom I was on
such excellent terms had not been commissioned by the G P.U. to
spy on me and hand them over a detailed report of everything I'd
said? The worst of it was that one could not even suspect the lack of
sincerity in one's friends. Russians are not particularly cunning by
nature, and everyone knows what a cult they make of friendship.
But, as Party members, we could not help knowing the methods of
the G.P.U., whose function it was to have detailed information about
everyone in any way connected with the intricate machinery of Soviet
bureaucracy. In my case, what more effective means could they find
than to order the very people with whom I was most intimate to
report on me? Moreover, the police were well aware that mere loyalty
to the regime was not a sufficient motive to their informers; they
had also to realize the terrible personal dangers that hung over their
own heads.

For instance: anyone who had been picked by the G.P.U. to make
a detailed weekly report on all my sayings and doings would never
dare to alter or gloss over the facts—for how was he to know that
there was not someone else carrying out the same orders? He knew
very well that the slightest tampering with the truth in his report would
infallibly land him in the appalling torture chambers of the G.P.U.
The mere fact of *not* discussing politics with one's friends would

have seemed suspicious to the terrible secret police. So, no matter what our real thoughts might be, whenever we were with friends or colleagues we all felt obliged to trot out a certain number of the current Party slogans. And this meant, of course, that there could never be any real, deep intimacy between friends, lovers, or even married couples.

It was, then, almost impossible for me to know what my companions really thought of Stalin's neo-imperialism and neo-patriotism: I could only guess at it from various telltale signs. It was not hard to discover, from the look and tone of certain students who by birth and tradition were pure Georgian, that they were in a state of suppressed revolt against this new offensive of the Russian imperialism which their forbears had fought so long and heroically. Still more noticeable were the general signs of horror and consternation when the great "purges" began. We were now asked to believe that the leaders of the revolution, Lenin's trusted companions, had, all along, been spies in the pay of capitalists and fascists. Yet what could we do but howl with the wolves?

I was finding the moral atmosphere of the Soviet Union harder to breathe every day. This was not only because I had lost my faith in Stalinist Communism. Even looked at objectively, from the purely Marxist standpoint, the whole regime seemed to be carrying on a competition in terrorism with Nazi Germany. More and more peasants were arrested for resisting collectivization, more and more factory workers accused of sabotage because they could not achieve impossible norms of production, arbitrarily fixed by a bureaucracy which, itself terrorized, was making frantic efforts to show its zeal. Throughout the whole length and breadth of the vast Soviet Union, men were living herded together behind barbed wire—that sign and symbol of a government which has lost all idea of freedom. Under an iron discipline enforced by the police, the victims of the concentration camps built factories, canals and new towns: cleared the steppes and forests. Being prisoners, they could not even bring the weapon of passive resistance to bear against the government's demands.

The fury of terrorism and persecution swept through every level of the Soviet population. There was hardly a week—hardly a day, perhaps—when I did not find that yet another colleague or student had disappeared. We, of course, carried on as though we saw nothing. The police themselves were afraid—afraid of seeming half-hearted. Whatever happened, they had to find enemies of the revolution; if they couldn't find them, they invented them.

THE HARD TASK OF A PROFESSOR

In this atmosphere of fear and distrust, my professorial work weighed on me unbearably. From the purely professional point of view I saw, the first time I set eyes on my students, that my task was going to be a thankless one, giving incomparably poorer results than would have been the case at any university in Western Europe Certain highly gifted students—and there were some—managed to surmount every obstacle and become outstanding scholars and technicians. But the level of general culture necessary to enter a faculty or advanced school was abnormally low—barely up to the standard of the French elementary diploma. University work was therefore bound to be very difficult to any student who was not exceptionally clever. Moreover, the propaganda slogans which had been dinned into the heads of the Soviet young ever since childhood had succeeded, in nearly all of them, in killing any disinterested curiosity they might ever have had. If a lecturer tried to interest his students in some writer or thinker, however famous, who had no visible connection with the immediate aims of socialist construction, they would at once denounce him to the G.P.U. He had committed the crime of "bourgeois formalism" and ran the risk of being sentenced for ideological deviationism. The regime was convinced that the only people it needed were technicians who could make themselves useful by carrying out its plans, and who never asked unnecessary questions. The result was that the students only wanted to learn what could be of immediate use to them. Professors of physics, chemistry, mathematics, and even literature and philosophy, were all training technicians and specialists.

The philosophy students too, then, were future "technicians"—technicians of propaganda. As soon as they started their course they knew that, barring some setback or purge, they would one day be working as secretaries to the Party or some syndicate, as propagandists in the Godless League, in a youth organization, or something of the sort. Most of them had been sent to the university by Party organizations which had already had reason to note their gift for agit-prop, and still more, their unquestioning obedience to orders. It was not surprising that my students showed even greater zeal than their colleagues in other faculties. Any deviationism which they might succeed in detecting in their professor or the other students would put them in the way of promotion and open the door to more important posts.

My work was to teach, in the light of historical materialism, the main trends of "bourgeois" philosophy. This might have been intensely interesting I had, as a Marxist, no objection to the principle of studying other philosophies and comparing them with Marxism. I should have liked to try to establish the political and economic contexts which had had a more or less direct influence on Plato, Descartes, Kant, Bergson and others. But this was not what my students expected of me. What did they care about the inner coherence of Bergsonism! As future teachers of Marxism to the Soviet peoples, all they were after was arguments in proof of the absolute superiority of Marxist-Leninism over all other philosophies, past, present and future. They had to be given the same kind of dogmatic instruction that one gets in a seminary. I was forced, therefore, to confine myself to giving them a clear and succinct account of the various philosophies, which I then went on to compare with Marxism, pointing out the different tricks by which one could prove that Marxism triumphantly refuted them all. What really mattered to these future "workers on the ideological front" (such was their official title) was to be able to make an impression on the masses whom they had to convince of the truth of Communism.

There could clearly be no question of my even suggesting that there might after all be some truth and beauty in these non-Marxist philosophies. At most, I would risk a few words in praise of some pre-Marxist thinker—and even then I was always careful to bring in a quotation from Engels, and to point out that, considering the economic conditions of his day, the philosopher in question was a progressive. Now, however, that Marx had brought the full and final enlightenment, it would be foolish to look for truth outside the works of his disciples and commentators. . . . Philosophers such as Bergson, James and Heidegger, who followed other lines of approach, *ipso facto* committed the most serious of all crimes against the mind —the crime of bourgeois idealism. It was the duty of a Marxist professor not merely to criticize but to condemn them—to prove that they were reactionaries, slavishly serving the interests of capitalism. Most Marxist writers on philosophy reserved special scorn for Bergson, whom they accused of dressing up a system of "spiritualist" mystification in a pseudo-scientific vocabulary.

A teacher of Marxist philosophy not only had to make out that Marx and Engels were of course philosophers of genius, but that Lenin, and even Stalin, were too. Woe to anyone who gave a lecture without finding some way of bringing in each of these authorities at least once. In the case of Lenin, it was not always easy, for although he was interested in philosophy, his own mind was somewhat shallow and very fragmentary. As for Stalin, the unfortunate professor had to be a real intellectual conjuror to produce any trace of philosophy from the few second-rate little books written by the accredited heir of Marxist truth. Yet, compared with my colleagues whose faculty was science, I had reason to regard myself as born under a lucky star. In philosophy it is always possible, with a little ingenuity, to find some quotation or other to fill the bill; whereas the other poor devils had to base their teaching of mechanics or botany on quotations from Lenin and Stalin.

THE WAR AGAINST RELIGION

I have already stressed more than once my complete lack of interest in everything to do with religion. Up to the time of which I write,

I had paid little attention to this aspect of Soviet life. Yet what would Kiev be, or Moscow, or Tiflis, without its cathedrals and monasteries? Or the humblest Russian village without its church? The fact that it was possible for me to stay and travel about in Russia without noticing any of this shows that I must have been so completely under the spell of Communism that I was unable to see anything save through its eyes. As soon as my own attitude changed, I could not fail to see all round me, not only the religious past of the country, but also its present.

Anyone who takes the trouble to consider Soviet citizens impartially has to admit that many years of anti-religious conflict, persecution, and "scientific" propaganda have not succeeded in alienating the Russian people from Christianity. It is true that almost all the churches, especially in the towns, are no longer used for worship; the finest of them have been turned into museums, the others into storerooms and so on. In Moscow, Leningrad and other large towns, a very few churches still have services held in them, to keep up the fiction of freedom of conscience. The only people one ever saw going into them were old men and women; the young all gave themselves out—if only from human respect—as atheists. It took the second World War to show how skin-deep this atheism was. When, in 1941, for reasons which do not concern this book, Stalin granted religious freedom to all Soviet citizens, the churches were invaded by young militant Communists, Red Army officers—all trained in the school of out-and-out atheistic materialism—asking to be baptized, or married with religious rites. It was obvious from this that the unconscious, at least, of Soviet youth had remained rooted in Christianity.

During my last stay in Russia the fight against religion was still being waged with tremendous zeal, especially in the country. The theoreticians of the regime, who did not understand the deep-seated reasons for the peasants' resistance to collectivization, fastened the responsibility for it on the lingering influence of the Church. It is certainly not necessary for me to write at length on the profound religious feeling of Russian peasants. Official atheism never stopped them from making their innumerable signs of the cross, or invoking God and the Mother of God on all possible occasions.

While in the Ukraine, I was once invited to take part in an expedition which a party of propagandists from the Godless League was about to make to a certain village. The local authorities had given orders that the peasants were to assemble in the House of the Soviet (roughly corresponding to a village hall). The speaker, a young student from Kharkov, made a long dissertation on the essential opposition between the darkness of religion as taught by the priests, and the scientific light of Stalinism. Another militant then read a resolution proposing that the village church should immediately be turned into a barn for the kolkhoz. All hands went up in a unanimous vote.

As we left, I congratulated the speaker on his dazzling success. He made a wry face and said, "Don't imagine it's the first time they've voted this way. Once a year, for the last ten years and more, the vote to close the churches is carried unanimously. Then, the moment we've left the village, the peasants run off to the priest and beg forgiveness for their 'sacrilege'—as they think it. Next Sunday, the church doors will stand open once more for their superstitious mumbo-jumbo. There's not a single peasant who'd have the pluck to put a sack of corn or potatoes in any building that had once been a church. Really, comrade, it's no joke trying to get the truth of science into the thick skulls of people with a thousand years of superstition behind them." The only thing that comforted the young man was the hope that the rising generation of peasants, brought up in Communist schools, would be more receptive of the truth. As we went along, talking, I looked back and there, sure enough, behind me was a line of men and women slowly making their way to the presbytery.

I couldn't help feeling interested when I found that every village still had its priest. Yet for years hardly a day had gone by without the Soviet press announcing that several priests had been arrested for "counter-revolutionary propaganda." I sought enlightenment on the point from various militant atheists. Their replies were usually evasive, and it was only gradually, by dovetailing all the bits of information I had collected, that I came to see how the Christian priesthood in the Soviet Union had been able to ensure its continuity.

All over Russia, in prisons and forced-labour camps there were not only priests but also many bishops, still carrying out their ministry, perhaps even more devotedly than they had once done in their own parishes or dioceses; it gives one courage to know that one is a martyr for one's faith. They were not, as a rule, allowed to celebrate Mass, but they prayed, and taught their companions in misfortune to pray—to turn to prayer for consolation and peace of mind. It happened fairly often that some moujik, sentenced to forced labour for failing to hand over the prescribed amount of corn, or killing his cattle rather than give them up to the kolkhoz, would receive quite a solid religious training while he was in captivity, and return home some years later as an ordained priest, ready to step into the shoes of some "pope" who had died or been deported during his absence. Several people assured me that thousands of ordinations and dozens of consecrations to the episcopate had taken place in Soviet prisons. Religious problems had no especial interest for me, but none the less I could not help feeling a certain admiration for the epic of the Russian Church. It was hard to resist the thought, especially when developments within the regime were taking such a disheartening turn, that in the new Russia the spiritual heirs of the characters in Gorki's *Mother,* to which I have referred so often, were none other than the believers.

My godless colleagues told me that, from their point of view, the most dangerous form of religion was not the Orthodox Church, for that was fairly easy to keep an eye on. For some years now, innumerable sects of varying degrees of eccentricity, some of them native products and others imported from abroad, had been spreading like wildfire through Russia, especially in country districts. They had no priesthood, and their followers met in private houses, where anyone who liked could teach or prophesy. These sects declared that the end of the world was at hand, identified the Soviet regime with the events of the Apocalypse, and made Stalin out to be antichrist.

The authorities held that the many fires which broke out in kolkhoz buildings and the assassination of several Communist leaders could all be put down to the state of ferment stirred up by these sects.

INTELLECTUAL PLANNING

I had long paid but little attention to the lack of intellectual freedom in the Soviet Union. I myself had voluntarily accepted Party orders as signposts in my literary and philosophical work, and it seemed to me perfectly natural that all branches of science, literature, art, music, and so forth, in the U.S.S.R. should likewise be subjected o strict Communist discipline. Nothing, I felt, could have less to say for itself than the principle of art for art's sake. Had not Lenin thus defined Communist morality: "Good is whatever serves the interest of the proletarian revolution; evil, whatever opposes it"? There could be no other criterion for the work of scientists, thinkers and artists

But, as I described in Chapter 4, for some years I had been fortunate enough to meet, fairly often, such men as Barbusse, Rolland, Unamuno and Zweig—to name only the most outstanding, and the dead. These great intellectuals were fighting, as I was, for the freedom of the people; some of them had even joined the Communist ranks. But how their culture overflowed the narrow limits of the textbooks! It never even crossed their minds that writers and thinkers, the better to serve the cause of revolution, should sacrifice the integrity of their own inspiration and their freedom of enquiry. This fact gave me plenty to think about.

Now that I no longer gasped with admiration at everything Soviet, I could not help seeing, with some consternation, what barbarians the "intellectuals" of the U.S.S R. were, compared with the great liberals of the West. The young, especially, were, with very few exceptions, completely unaware that any contribution had ever been made by the West to philosophy and science Moreover—and this, to me, seemed even more serious—they showed no intellectual interest in anything that happened outside Russia. They accepted it as a sort of revealed dogma that only the Soviet Union could give great artists and scientists the conditions they needed if they were to flourish: that nothing of value could ever again come out of a capitalist country. Such chauvinistic sectarianism seemed a terribly far cry from the universalism which I had always regarded as the essence of true Communist thought.

It did not take me long to see the disastrous results of rigidism in the intellectual sphere. Up to about 1930, Soviet artists and scientists had had almost unrestricted freedom—assuming, of course, that they did nothing counter-revolutionary. It was in those days that Cholokov wrote his novel *And Quiet Flows the Don,* which it is no exaggeration to call a masterpiece. In it, he described the ups-and-downs of the Civil War in a Cossack village on the Don. Then, some time later, Stalin insisted that all intellectuals must become "fighters on the ideological front." From thenceforth it was the Politburo that chose the subjects for writers and artists. They were not even allowed complete freedom in matters of style. Cholokov, like Gladkov, Fedin and other writers of undeniable talent, all toed the line. But, alas, although his novel on the Civil War had been a piece of great literature, *The Earth,* which he botched up on Party orders, to boost the kolkhozes, was no more than second-rate journalism. And what I have said of Cholokov was true of all the others. Even genius seemed powerless to shake off the chains that Stalin and Idanov had laid on the human mind.

In public squares, at exhibitions, in meeting-halls, there were endless statues and pictures of Stalin, his faithful henchmen, and perhaps some stakhanovite or other; or else there might be a scene of collective life in a factory or kolkhoz. Some of them were signed by artists whose work one had admired in the past, but even they seemed to have lost all creative gift.

Only the theatre appeared not to have come off too badly at the hands of the intellectual planners. True, it had to put on more and more plays forced on it by the headquarters of agit-prop, all glorifying collectivism, the Red Army, or industrialism. But Russians are born actors, and many of the cast managed to give a personal and moving touch to even a fifth-rate piece of propaganda.

Despite the ill effects of rigidism, artists were probably the only people in the various categories of the Soviet population whose interior life had not been brought to a complete standstill, and who still speculated about the meaning and value of life. Anyone who has read the great Russian novelists knows how profoundly preoccupied the whole race is by the question of the beyond. Indeed, no people on earth is less fitted by nature to be the heralds of materialism, of *homo economicus.* The favourite word of every Russian is certainly "soul"; but for Communists there is no soul. Nor may any Communist have an inner life, or ever listen to the voice of conscience. It is the Party which tells him what to do and think. The leaders of the Party take to themselves—not, of course, in theory, but in practice always—a general infallibility which even the Pope does not possess in the eyes of loyal Catholics.

Communism has not succeeded in turning all Russians into robots. Even Party members have held out better than one might have expected. All the same, I had many opportunities of seeing for myself how almost all the intellectuals refused to touch anything that had the slightest tincture of metaphysical speculation: the only questions they ever seemed to ask themselves were those to which the Party held the answers. Such docility can be explained to a great extent by the fact that almost all these new intellectuals were of working-class or peasant origin, whose parents, more often than not, were illiterate: they themselves, in many cases, had not learnt to read and write until they were adults. The passion for learning of these men and women is quite staggering: in no country in the world, speaking proportionately, are so many books, reviews and newspapers read as in the U S.S.R. But at that time they were intellectual adolescents. The teaching they were given—even the fearfully rudimentary teaching doled out by the Soviet schools and universities—satisfied their mental needs. They drank it in without any thought of criticism, as meekly as their parents and grandparents had swallowed the marvels in pilgrims' tales. It will take time—perhaps a long time—before these intellectuals, or rather their sons and grandsons, come to see how much in science is relative, how little is certain. Then, too, they will at last understand that dialectic is not capable of solving *all* the problems that beset the mind of man.

And yet, between 1930 and 1935, I met several painters, sculptors and actors who were beginning to have some confused sense of the narrowness and inadequacy of the official teaching. They were, I could see, uneasy in their minds, gropingly speculating on the deeper meaning of art and the ultimate significance of their own existence.

GOOD-BY TO THE U.S.S.R.

At the stage which I had now reached, life in the Soviet Union held nothing for me. I had lost my faith, and everything that I had to do and teach was now simply a burden, and a burden which grew heavier every day. I longed to protest, to cry aloud my anger at the men whom I thought guilty of betraying the revolution. But I knew the merciless cruelty of the regime well enough to realize that any sign of disillusionment on my part would be suicidal—nor would it have the faintest chance of opening the eyes of anyone else.

For the same reason, it was out of the question for me to think of leaving the Party, that I might no longer share in its work of betrayal. There is no private life for a Soviet citizen—still less for a Party member. Besides, the advantages of belonging to the Party were so great that if I had given them up of my own free will I should have been taken for a dangerous lunatic As I have already said, the Party does not recognize the right of anyone to scruples of conscience; nor does it admit the right of neutrality. One is for or against: if one has ceased to be for, one can only be against, and will, logically enough, be treated with the severity which is the portion of all counter-revolutionaries. That a Communist should, in all sincerity and as a matter of conviction, change his political views, is, to a Marxist, quite inconceivable Had I left the Party, the Party could only have concluded, with the logic peculiar to it, that I had never been a real Communist: that I was a traitor and spy, all along.

Now that I was no longer convinced of the absolute infallibility and excellence of Stalin's regime, I found my vision becoming clearer and more critical every day. It grew increasingly difficult for me to act a part, or pretend to a conviction and enthusiasm which I no longer felt. But what was I to do?

Fortunately, at that time, the door leading from the Red paradise was not so firmly shut as it was some years later. One was even allowed to correspond with people abroad. A "Congress for World Peace" was about to take place in London, and I was able to get myself officially invited. Armed with this invitation, I applied for an exit visa, and, to my great amazement, got it. But not until I had crossed the frontier of the Soviet Union did I feel myself a free man. And this sense of freedom was incomparably more intense than any I had ever felt on leaving prison.

What was I to make of this freedom? I had for so long been leading a life completely given up to a great ideal that it was out of the question for me now to settle down to what is usually thought of as normal existence—to practise a profession, found a family, and so on. For years I had been outspoken in my arrogant contempt for what I was later to call the daily round, as opposed to authentic existence. I had broken with the Communist party, certainly, but I had no intention of being untrue to myself.

Besides, I was still strongly attached to the Communist ideal. How, indeed, could it be imagined that I should suddenly turn my back on all I had lived for, for so many years? Many militant Communists broke with the Party at about that time. I believed, as they all did, that the reason I was so deeply disappointed in the Soviet Union, and felt I had no alternative but to leave the Party, was that Stalin and his clique had betrayed true Communism. I was as sure as I had ever been that in itself Communism was good. I therefore got in touch with Trotsky, Victor Sergeii and several other leaders of what was known as the Communist opposition of the Left. I even wrote several articles in Trotskyist publications, and meant to write, with Victor Sergeii, a book on the Revolution Betrayed.

I soon had to admit to myself that the shock I had had in the U.S.S.R. had been too much for me. Stalin's dictatorship had seemed so terribly solid. I found it hard to believe that Trotsky and the rest of the opposition, with the means, or lack of means, at their disposal, could do anything effective to salvage the revolution once it had been betrayed. I was well aware of Stalin's extraordinary cunning. He would suggest pacts of peaceful coexistence to capitalist governments with a show of good will that increased in proportion to the amount of opposition he was up against inside the U.S.S.R. The opposition had no hope of any support from without. Besides, the "incorruptibles" in control of it would never have agreed to an alliance with the enemies of Communism, even if they had thought that Communism would thereby be saved. The Kremlin even induced most of the capitalist governments to institute a policy of petty persecution against the refugees of the opposition. I grew discouraged, and gradually slipped away even from Trotskyist circles.

STALIN DID NOT BETRAY

It was not until my powers of philosophic thought had achieved more maturity, and I was able to see the years I spent in the Party in the perspective given them by distance, that I could form a truer picture of what had happened in Russia. Today I am quite convinced that Stalin and his followers did not betray the ideology of Marx and Lenin, but remained, perhaps almost unconsciously, true to the fundamental teaching of their masters. Probably, indeed, if they had been less faithful to the basic principles of Marxism, the Russian people would have had less to suffer and would not now be a mortal danger to the essential freedom of mankind.

The crimes of Communism are due, not to the wickedness of those at the head of it, but to the materialism and denial of all transcendent values which are its chief characteristics. In Marx's own words, man had become the supreme being for man; and as, in

Marxist eyes, he is only, when all is said and done, a being more highly evolved than any other, he was inevitably crushed beneath the inhuman social machine. Marxist Communism stands faithfully by the old Hegelian principle which maintains that the universal alone has true reality, and the particular exists only as a function of the universal. There can, therefore, logically, be no hesitation whenever a conflict arises between what, to Communists, is the universal *par excellence*—the Communist State—and the welfare of individuals—even the vast majority of individuals who make up that State. As all sentiment is banned on principle, there is nothing to stop Communism from enslaving, humiliating and degrading individuals whenever it seems to the State's interests to do so. It does not even hesitate to sling mud at its best servants, if occasion arises. It did so in a big way during the notorious trials of the veterans of the Revolution—Zinoviev, Kamenev, Rykov and the rest, who were made to accuse themselves, before the People's Tribunal, of being the vile spies of capitalist imperialism. Still more recently, the terrible head of the political police, Beria, was sentenced to death as a spy and traitor. Materialistic Communism is quite unconcerned by the fact that, to those who believe the prosecution, this gives a very disturbing picture of men who were looked on as the leading representatives of Communism. All that matters is results.

A slightly more subtle way of degrading Communist man is to make him renounce his ideal of serving humanity unselfishly by holding out the lure of personal gain as the only motive both for his activity and for the much-talked-of "socialist emulation." The same end is achieved in the case of writers, artists, scientists and philosophers by insisting that they should renounce all free inspiration and become the tools of propaganda.

Quite certainly, Stalin and his colleagues and successors never consciously set themselves to degrade man. But to them, man as an individual was never sufficiently interesting to be bothered about. The German concentration camps and the Russian forced-labour camps, whatever their superficial resemblances, came into being for entirely different reasons. The Nazis worked with the express purpose of degrading their adversaries within the State—Jews, and others of racial origins which they considered inferior. The Russian camps, like the "voluntary" confessions and the intellectual servility in Russia and other countries under Communist rule, grew out of Marxist metaphysics as the oak grows out of the acorn. Communism could, of course, if it liked, put an end to the system of forced-labour camps, and even to the trials of "spies" and "traitors." If its reason for doing so was that the interests of the State demanded it, it would still be true to itself. But if ever, out of respect for human dignity, it were to stop degrading man, it would be flouting its own principles.

6 *Light in Darkness*

In the preceding chapters I have been careful to stress my complete lack of any kind of religious life or religious interests during my years as a militant Communist, and even before I joined the Young Communists. I know that those who have been believers from their earliest childhood will find this surprising, but it is none the less true that up to the time of which I am now writing no sort of religious anxiety had ever troubled me. I had never seriously asked myself what would become of me when I was dead; but it went beyond that—the question held no interest for me at all. Life on earth, in the dimension of time, was so absorbing, there was so much to be done, that anything outside this seemed quite futile. And I was not, as I need hardly say, a rare case. I don't think I am wrong in saying that the great majority of Communists, and of educated atheists in general, are as little concerned with the problem of the after-life as I was up to the age of twenty-six. To me and all my comrades it was an understood thing that death came as the final end of the individual—that our life and death, in the last analysis, could be of use only to the race. This in no way prevented our having an ardent love for this fleeting existence; quite the contrary. Besides, those of us who, like myself, were Hegelians to the marrow of our bones, thought it quite natural that the particular—that is, the individual—should be sacrificed to the universal—in other words, humanity as a whole.

CHRISTIANITY THROUGH THE EYES OF ANATOLE FRANCE

Just once, however, when I was about sixteen or seventeen, I had found religion beautiful and moving. I was reading *Thaïs*, by that most brilliant eclectic of our time, Anatole France, who, for somewhat strange reasons, became a Communist in his old age. As he belonged to the Party, I did not feel it my duty to summon up that *a priori* distrust that we usually felt of all bourgeois writers whose books we had to read for the sake of our work. I have not reread *Thaïs,* and therefore cannot say what impression it would make on me now. I know that Christians generally find it utterly irreligious. I think myself that if I were to read it again, my strongest impression would be that it rang false. But the young Communist that I then was felt that he was reading a very Christian book, or at least a book very much in sympathy with the Christianity of the first century.

I don't remember the name of the holy hermit who, in the solitude of his desert, heard of Thaïs, the notorious Alexandrian courtesan. He thought he heard a voice from God telling him to go to the great city and there convert this woman who was doing so much harm. More obedient than Jonas, off he went. He found Thaïs, and, in holy wrath, threatened her with the flames of hell. She laughed in his face and carried her impudence to such a pitch that she actually tried her blandishments on him. The irate hermit called down curses on her, and then went back to his desert. But he could not forget her face, or her provocative laugh. For years he subjected himself to appalling austerities. But the obsession increased every day, until the time came when he could hold out no longer. Again he left the desert and for many days walked towards Alexandria—not, this time, to threaten the sinner with hell-fire, but to share her sin. When he reached Alexandria, he found the streets thronged with a vast, joyful procession of Christians. What was it all about? He soon heard: they were celebrating the canonization of Thaïs, once a sinner. While he himself had been battling with temptation in his desert, the words he had sown in her soul had borne fruit. She was converted, and became a great saint.

This story that Anatole France invented—although, as I heard later, it had some historical foundation—is not free from that libidinous sentimentality which was one of his characteristics. It contains so much that is indecent that preachers and moralists have some justification for condemning it. But at that time I knew nothing of any moral criteria. Besides, despite my boasted materialism, when I was young I craved the romantic, probably because I had so little of it in my own life. As *Thaïs* was the work of a Communist, I felt I need have no scruples about being carried away by its charm. And unless my memory is playing me false, it still seems to me that the author was not far out in his interpretation of the mysterious communion between the holy monk and the beautiful courtesan. However, my admiration was purely aesthetic. I had no wish to imitate either the monk in his mortifications or Thaïs in her conversion. The words "sin" and "temptation" were mere abstract ideas to me, unrelated to anything definite on the existential plane.

EXPERIENCE OF AN ABSURD FORM OF EXISTENCE

The day on which I tore up my Party card, I had no thought of Anatole France's novel. I should certainly have been annoyed—unless, indeed, the idea had merely struck me as ridiculous—if anyone had taken it into his head to tell me that I myself should one day undergo religious conversion. For ten years I had lived entirely by and for Communist ideals. I had never imagined my life otherwise than as given up, body and soul, to the cause of revolution. It is true that I had taken the trouble to widen and deepen my cultural interests as much as I could, and collect diplomas. But I told myself that this was simply that I might have the right equipment for the work entrusted to me by the Party—just as, when I was an adolescent, I had dreamed of becoming a famous writer or philosopher. I quite believed that personal vanity had ceased to play any part in my ambitions. I had seen for myself the extraordinary influence of books like Gorki's and Barbusse's: could I find any more excellent way of serving the Cause than by making myself as like them as possible?

All these years I had been living what was, to all intents and purposes, the life of an ascetic. This was not due to moral principles— I hadn't any—but simply because I was afraid that women, drink and tobacco would lessen my usefulness as a revolutionary and dis-

tract me from what I looked on as all-important. Even today I don't
find it easy to believe in "natural virtue." Some years ago I heard
a priest, with a scientific training behind him, say in a sermon: "Even
if God did not exist, it would still be our duty to live chaste, sober
and decent lives, for these are the outcome of the natural virtues."
I confess that this idea is beyond me. It is true that one does not
have to believe in God in order to lead a chaste, sober and decent
life. But one must at least believe in some ideal—an ideal which,
psychologically speaking, has become a kind of idol—if one is to
submit to the restraints demanded by what we know as virtue Nothing seems to me further from a truly existential—and therefore
Christian—outlook than this faith in "natural goodness," which owes
far more to Rousseau than to the Gospels.

Be that as it may, I myself no longer believed that Communism
was the supreme, historical, concrete ideal, or that it was capable of
leading mankind towards "singing morrows." As long as my faith
was intact, life was a thing of beauty to me, and no sacrifice or
restraint too great. Now I could not think what to do with myself.
What was the good of living and working if one had no further
motive for doing so? I knew of course that there were men—probably
the majority of men—who felt no need to justify their existence—to
find in it, or to give it, a sense and meaning. A daily round, which
has little connection with real living, comes quite naturally to them,
and it never even occurs to them to look for anything further. They
are born, eat, drink, work, have children and die, with almost as few
problems as animals. They are completely natural. God forbid that
I should think myself better than they, but the fact remains that I
have always been different.

At that time no one had heard of Jean Paul Sartre But I needed
no philosophical justification for thinking that my life had now become utterly absurd—as completely aimless as a stone or a tree. I
flung myself frantically into all the pleasures and amusements which
until then I had always felt it my duty to give up. I did indeed find
some kind of forgetfulness of all that was causing me such anguish,
but it was a forgetfulness as short-lived as a state of intoxication. I

suppose I was too unused to that sort of life and lacked the necessary zest for it, for my bouts of pleasure were followed by an apathy and revulsion worse than anything that had gone before. Not everyone has it in him to be dissolute Life at that time seemed so pointless that suicide looked like the only way out. I thought of it seriously, and even attempted it several times. But my instinctive clinging to life was stronger than I should have cared to admit—which makes me think that, contrary to what Sartre says, it is disgust with life which contains a considerable dose of bad faith.

Then it occurred to me to get back at least part of my father's legacy, which I had brushed aside in so lordly a manner. I pictured myself living, almost monastically, in a small house that I should have had built for myself on something as near as I could get to a desert island. Here I should devote myself to the ennobling labours of scholarship, and write books. But my ten years of intensive life as a militant Communist had left a deep and lasting mark on me. In any case, I had probably always been by temperament a man of action. No doubt it was reaction against my family background—which contained *only* men of action—that made me imagine, during the crises of adolescence, that solitude had any charms for me. However plunged in despair I might be, I could not help knowing in my heart that I was no more cut out for the peaceful existence of a hermitscholar than I was for a life of debauchery. I should certainly have been unable to write anything whatever unless I was spurred on by the urgent wish to convey some message to other people.

Still less did I feel myself fitted for an everyday life—getting married and practising a profession like everybody else. I had always felt contemptuous of "bourgeois life," and to go in for it now would have seemed a worse comedown than any loose living. I knew that many people regarded me as an excellent teacher and would have advised me to take up teaching, which I had always loved, as a profession. But teaching, too, seemed to me inconceivable except as a means of transmitting a message in which I myself believed ardently. I now believed in nothing, and therefore had nothing to communicate. Nor, in my case, could love for a woman ever come to be a motive for living. Love, in its aspect of a storm in a sealed jar, had always seemed to me futile and ridiculous. During my life as a militant, love had given me an overflow of energy, enthusiasm and generosity for the conflict. But what should I now do with the joy and impetus it would bring? It would give me, not peace and certainty, but only anguish and dissatisfaction.

"QUO VADIS, DOMINE?"

There I was, then, in a state of complete mental confusion, when the Sign was shown me.

It was late at night. I had just got back from one of the *soi-disant* artists' clubs where I spent all my evenings. The general atmosphere and outlook in them was more or less identical with what one knows only too well of the "cellars" near St. Germain-des-Prés since the second World War. Gide and Malraux, Picasso and Breton were discussed with more vehemence than conviction. It was the fashion to stand out against any commitment which would entail the least restriction of what these snobs called their "freedom." Above all, everyone drank a lot; and the girls, even more than the men, announced themselves as completely emancipated from all principles and morality. Naturally enough, I found it all completely empty, but at least I wasn't alone, and I could benumb myself with unreality.

On this occasion the hands of my watch must have pointed to three or four in the morning by the time I reached home. But, as often happened now, I could not go to sleep. To fill in the time, I looked on the drawing-room table for the novel which my host's daughter had left there. At first I glanced through it absent-mindedly, for books no longer had enough interest for me to make me forget the fundamental emptiness of existence. That night, however, for the first time for months, a novel did succeed in holding my attention— succeeded so well, indeed, that I forgot about the Communist Party and my own despair, how tired I was and how late it was getting. I identified myself with the hero almost as I had done ten years before when I read *Mother:* really, I should never have believed I was still so young! Books had always been my best friends. They had given me an indispensable means of getting away from the limitations of everyday life; they had shown me a more subtle form of thinking, and brought to light the hidden longings of my own soul. Nevertheless, especially since I had become literary critic for several papers and reviews, I had always refused to identify myself with the heroes of the novels I was reading; that would really have been rather too childish! I always tried to read with the greatest possible detachment —the objectivity which I felt befitted a Marxist. I even made it a rule to stop reading any novel the minute I felt I was being carried away by it.

That night I did not try to curb my wish for escapism. On the contrary, I was delighted to be able, for a few hours, to exchange the drabness of my own life for the lives of other people.

By the time I at last finished the book and laid it down, it was midday. My eyes were filled with tears. I was hardly conscious of feeling tired, after a whole night without sleep. It was not until I had finished the book that I looked at its title—*Quo Vadis?*, by a certain Sienkiewicz. The *Petit Larousse* informed me that he was a Polish novelist who had won the Nobel Prize in 1905. I had never heard of him.

I expect that most of my readers know *Quo Vadis?*, so that it will not be necessary for me to describe its plot at any length. It is a historical novel, very much in the style of the late nineteenth century, and set in the age of Nero, when a savage persecution of Christians was raging in the imperial capital. The followers of Christ, one after another, were flung to the lions in the circus, or set on fire and left to blaze like torches, to light up the festivities in the Emperor's gardens. Some, like their Master, were crucified. The apostle Paul was put to death, and Peter, the Prince of the Apostles, began, as once before, to waver. He let himself be persuaded that he would be serving the best interests of the Church if he fled. But, when he had left the city walls behind him, he met Christ, walking towards Rome. "Where art Thou going, Lord?" he asked in consternation: "*Quo vadis, Domine?*" Christ's reply was uncompromising: "As you, Peter, are deserting My flock, I am going to Rome, to be crucified for the second time." No more was needed to make the apostle repent of his cowardice. He turned back, took his place once more at the head of the community, and, not long after, was crucified. On his own plea, as a mark of humility, he was fastened to the cross head downwards.

If I had not been so totally ignorant of everything connected with Christianity, it is quite likely that Sienkiewicz's novel would have made less impression on me. Even as it was, there were many things in it which I did not understand. Why, for instance, was it so important that Peter should die *in Rome?* Again, I did not see the true significance of his meeting with Christ. These were matters I was as yet unable to understand, for they belonged to the supernatural order whose very existence was a closed book to me. What I found so enthralling in *Quo Vadis?* was the picture it gave of the life of Christian communities in the first century I felt suddenly as if everything for which I had been confusedly longing ever since I was fifteen, and had vainly sought in Communism, was not, at all, to be found only in some imaginary Utopia. The early Christians had made it come true.

The fact that the book was a novel, not a work of strict historical accuracy, did not at once strike me. As soon as I did realize that it was, after all, a work of the imagination, I made up my mind to find out at all costs whether, and to what extent, Sienkiewicz had respected the truth of history, or whether this was just another bit of propaganda writing on the pattern of the books meekly turned out by Communists at the orders of the Politburo. I knew, for instance, how very little resemblance there was between the kolkhoz of the Russian novel and the kolkhoz of real life. Had the Polish novelist also been turning out clever propaganda with only a very flimsy basis of reality?

Some readers may feel surprised that a book, and a novel at that, should once again play so important a part in my life. To understand it, they should remember that reading and writing had always been my keenest pleasure, as well as my own personal way of sharing the conflicts and sufferings of others.

AT THE SOURCES OF CHRISTIANITY

For weeks after I read *Quo Vadis?* I never went near any of my clubs. I didn't mind, for I had never really felt at home in them.

I went to the public library and began by drawing up a list of all the books which dealt with the first three centuries of Christian history. Then I set to work systematically to read them. First came the novels, for I have always held that a good novelist can feel himself into the spirit of a given period even better than a learned historiographer. Everything was grist to my mill—Lord Lytton's *The Last Days of Pompeii,* then Cardinal Wiseman's *Fabiola,* then French, German and Italian novels on the same theme. Not all the authors were of the same religion: indeed, some of them obviously had no Christian faith at all Yet it was significant that they all agreed on essentials.

By the time I had finished reading these novels, I was already fairly at home in the atmosphere and "climate" of primitive Christianity. I next set about tackling more serious works, beginning with Renan's *Vie de Jésus,* which one of the librarians had recommended. I did not as yet see that Renan's "history" was at least as novelesque as the novels. I thought it very beautiful, and felt a deep sympathy with the hero, the "gentle Jesus of smiling Galilee." How well I understood all those men and women, who had only to see Him and hear Him call them by name, and they at once left home, work and family to follow Him! The fact that Renan denied His divinity did not trouble me at all. I was not looking for a god, only for a new ideal of life— in time, and on this earth. What Jesus taught, and His own way of living, seemed to me extremely beautiful.

From Renan, I went on to historians who kept a tighter rein on their imaginations and stuck more closely to the facts. I devoured, pellmell, the works of rationalists—Harnack, Strauss, Guignebert, Loisy—of the Protestant Sabatier, and of Catholics such as Batiffol, Duchesne, Prat and Lagrange. Here again, I hardly noticed any divergencies. What did I care for discussions on the exact meaning of some saying of Christ's, or the discrepancies, great or small, between accounts of the same events as narrated by different evangelists? In everything which, to me, was essential, I felt that all the various authors were in wonderful agreement. Could one imagine Stalin, Trotsky, Zinoviev and Rykov writing almost identical histories of the October Revolution and the founding of the Soviet Union? Yet Catholics, Protestants and unbelievers all painted the first Christian community in almost the same colours. What was one to deduce from this, if not that they were all drawing on the same source, a source of incontestable historical truth?

It was true, then, that a certain teaching had been dynamic enough to weld men of all races and conditions into one brotherly community —to fill the gulf which separated master from slave. I thought it magnificent, superhuman, that the Church should honour as saints both princes and slaves. I found that underlying this Christian community, too, there was a dialectic, but a dialectic based on universal love. And I had to admit that, on the sociological plane which alone interested me, it could point to better results than the dialectic of the class struggle, which had led to nothing but the substitution, for the former ruling class, of a dictatorship at least equally pitiless.

After some weeks, I felt that I had a fairly good idea of the structure based on the teaching of Jesus of Nazareth. All the authors I had read referred to the same source—the Gospels. So I went into the first bookshop I came across and bought a copy of the New Testament. I was surprised to see what a small book it was. That same day I read at a sitting the four Gospels and the Acts. The Epistles and Apocalypse seemed to me more hermetic and of less importance: I did no more than skim through them. The miracles, and all the marvellous side of the life of Christ and the apostles, were a source of embarrassment to me. From that first day I learnt for myself what I have since proved true a hundred times over—that miracles, which used to be regarded as the chief guarantee of the truth of Christianity, are today its main stumbling block. The hagiographers, and the popular imagination of the Middle Ages, used to invent miracles to chalk up to the credit of their favourite saints. Everyone felt that there were not enough miracles in the Gospels, and so apocryphas came to be written, attributing to Christ what to us seem mere fairy-tale marvels. The educated man of today wishes that the Gospels contained no accounts of miracles at all. Far from looking on them as a motive for believing in Him, our contemporaries do not accept the miracles unless they already have faith. I do not mean to imply that we are right and that our ancestors were wrong. I am merely stating a fact to which catechists and others should give due weight.

To me, the accounts of Christ's miracles—which I thought very lovely—seemed to belong to a literary *genre* which has produced many masterpieces, starting with the *Odyssey*. I classified the folklore of all races, with their myths and legends, under the same heading. As, in principle, I had nothing against this type of literature, I was not in the least surprised to find so many miracles in the life of Christ. I simply paid no attention to them for the time being. What was important was the sublimity of Christ's teaching, by which, even at this first reading of the Gospel, I was completely overcome. The Sermon on the Mount, for instance: how incomparably more beautiful it was than the Communist Manifesto! Then, again, the parables; they were not only full of poetry, but conveyed the most wonderful doctrine. But nothing in the Gospels impressed me so much as the character of Christ Himself. His simplicity, His inexhaustible kindness to all who were suffering, the terms of perfect equality He accepted, not only among His disciples but with the poorest of His people—all this was a marvellous confirmation of His teaching in the Sermon on the Mount and the parables. How very different was His treatment of sinners—Mary of Magdala, the woman taken in adultery, the publicans—from the police methods in force in the Soviet Union!

When I had finished reading the Gospels I could no longer doubt that the life of the Christian community described by the historians and novelists I had been reading was directly inspired by the teaching of Christ. The Acts of the Apostles showed me that there was a direct link between the small group of men and women clustered round Christ Himself, and the Christian communities that flourished hundreds of years later in Rome, Alexandria, Asia Minor and Gaul. The author of the Acts taught me something I had never heard before—that in Jerusalem just after Pentecost "all they that believed were together and had all things in common," and that "their possessions and goods they sold and divided them to all, according as everyone had need." Was not this in line with the purest ideals of Communism? To me, it was a reference of capital importance. It is true that I was bitterly disappointed by the way Marxist Communism had worked out in Russia, but I was none the less convinced that the ideal of Communism was the finest and most generous in the world, and that, if only there were some other way of realizing it than by the methods which had been adopted in Russia, it could bring nothing but happiness to mankind. My opinion of any philosophical doctrine or social policy depended almost entirely on its degree of conformity with Communist ideals. The ideal society described in Plato's *Republic* is admittedly not entirely like the society of the modern socialist's dream, but it was none the less communist, and that alone was enough to make me rate Plato above all the other philosophers of antiquity. And what attracted me to Christianity was the fact that the teaching, and the practical realization of the teaching, of Christ and His followers, was "communistic." Not until much later did all the rest come to be added to this first concept—a "rest" which is no doubt far more fundamental in the Christian synthesis than what I had first admired.

Even now that I have a better understanding of Christianity, I still take my stand against people who feel called upon to flare up whenever anyone speaks of the "communism" of Christ and the first Christian communities. Their indignation would only be justified if the word "communist" could be used in one sense alone, and that a strictly dogmatic one. Christ and His followers were not, needless to say, aiming at a totalitarian dictatorship, nor yet at the enforced expropriation of property—still less at setting up a Moloch State to crush the human personality. Yet I am far from being the only man, or the first, to have felt, on reading the Gospels, that the social ideal of Christianity was communistic. No one, of course, not even a disciple, was *obliged* to give up all his property and live in community. St. Peter stated this quite clearly to Ananias, who had in fact entered a community and then defrauded it of part of his goods: "Why hath Satan tempted thy heart that thou shouldst lie to the Holy Ghost and by fraud keep part of the price of the land? Whilst it remained, did it not remain to thee? And, after it was sold, was it not in thy power?" The Christian "communists" felt no hatred for those in the other camp, and there was complete democracy in their communities. If then, one sets the practical "communism" of the Christian communities up against the practical Communism of the Marxists, one sees that no comparison is possible. On the other hand, when one studies the psychological content of the ideal of each, one cannot fail to see that the two have much in common. The labour camps, the police dictatorship and other characteristics of the Soviet regime, hold no place in the minds of the great majority of those who, dazzled by the Communist ideal, have joined the Party. They accept these abuses because they have been persuaded—or have persuaded themselves—that for the time being such things are necessary in the name of historical imperatives.

Nothing, therefore, seems to me more unfair than to take the Soviet regime as the prototype of Communism and use it as a pattern by which all other forms of Communism must be judged. All the sincere Communists whom I have known well have cherished dreams of a kind of society of brothers which, if they could have their way, would probably not be so very different from the first Christian communities. I feel, then, that it would be fairer to regard these Christian communities as having come nearest to the realization of the true Communist ideal. We should then be driven to the conclusion that the Soviet Union had merely annexed the Communist label: that the Communism of the Marxist, by the mere fact that it had rejected Christianity, could not be genuine.

This was how I looked on all these matters after my first reading of the New Testament.

It would have been quite foreign to my nature and active temperament to waste much time passively admiring the early Christian communities. I was not living under Nero or Diocletian. I had to justify my existence in the complex society of the twentieth century, in Western Europe. Was it only one period of history which had had the Christian ideal as its very soul? Was this ideal, to us, no more than a moving and beautiful memory, as Marx had held? Or had it resisted the corrupting touch of time, to inspire those who still followed it? If so, surely this was the one ideal capable of satisfying the longings, however vague and undefined they might be, of the best men of our day?

There was as yet no question of my believing in the resurrection of Christ. To me this was just a beautiful symbol, which I thought could be applied on the sociological plane. It was, therefore, a matter of major importance to me to verify the authenticity of the symbol. If Christ's teaching still bore fruit in the social life of mankind, I should think it perfectly reasonable to talk of His victory over death, and find no difficulty in agreeing that He Himself was alive. To me as an Hegelian, individual life counted for very little.

If, on the other hand, all that was left of the Christian community was a memory of long ago, then the Man of Galilee would be just one more of those great men, such as Socrates, Confucius, Seneca, Marx and Tolstoi, who have bequeathed to the world some noble teaching, but failed to endow this teaching with any lasting life. In that case the resurrection of Christ would be a lie.

My hopes of finding a *living* Christ were not very strong. I had heard all too much from the Marxists of the Church's complicity with the injustices of the established order. Christ was always said to be on the side of the poor and oppressed, but those who claimed to speak in His name taught them that their chief duty lay in resignation—a resignation which played into the hands of the rich and powerful. I was afraid that contemporary Christianity might bear even less resemblance to the Gospels than Stalin's regime bore to the ideal for which I had lived so long. But I didn't think it a good policy to deliver a verdict before I had verified the facts for myself. Then, too, I myself longed to prove from my enquiry that mankind was not up against a brick wall.

A LIGHTNING TOUR AMONG THE SECTS

I looked up the various Christian communities of our day in an encyclopedia: never should I have believed that there were so many, and all so different! From the accounts given in the encyclopedia, it seemed to be the non-conformists or "eccentrics" who had most in common with the early Christian communities. The events at Jerusalem on and after the day of Pentecost were not, after all, themselves without a touch of eccentricity—nor, indeed, was the life of Christ. This did not worry me, for it was conformity much more than eccentricity that had always got on my nerves.

For several weeks I turned up assiduously at the meetings of the Baptists, Methodists, Adventists, and many others of the sects that swarmed in the country where I was then living. I was deeply moved by the fervour of the men and women I saw at these meetings. Among one sect in particular I witnessed scenes of collective ecstasy which must, I felt, be very like those described in the Acts. There could be no doubt about it: to these people, most of them obviously in humble circumstances, Jesus of Nazareth was not just one of the illustrious dead. They talked to Him as though He were really there, as though He could hear and answer them. This didn't fit in any too well with my theory of a symbolical resurrection, but I didn't bother much about that.

After these meetings, I usually asked to see the Pastor-Preacher of the community. I always told him who I was and what I was looking for, and asked him to tell me about his Church. I was almost always taken aback by the intellectual mediocrity of the men I talked to. They admitted that they could not answer my questions with any degree of exactness, and seemed far too ready to shelter behind the inexplicable nature of what they called a "mystery." Then, too, there was the strange intolerance of these men of God, otherwise so pious and charitable, towards all other Churches—especially the Church that they referred to, scathingly, as "Papist." This was something even worse than the intolerance of Communists: it showed me the true meaning of the word "sectarian." If one were to believe them, then the Church of whatever man I was speaking to at the moment was the only one to know the truth and to hold the keys of heaven. I didn't know the Gospels well, but this was not the impression they had given me. Besides, all these pious folk seemed pretty indifferent over the question of improving the earthly conditions of humanity.

But there was another matter which to me was still more serious. With my philosophical education, based on Hegel, I believed firmly in History, and had no respect for anything but the universal. Everything that was specifically sectarian in these sects naturally seemed to me the negation of the universal. The preachers usually referred to the salvation of the individual soul, and it certainly looked at the prayer meetings as if this salvation were the main concern of the faithful. Now, I was wholly indifferent to the salvation of my soul: the question presented no problem to me.

On the historical level, I was anxious to establish the continuity between the community grouped round Christ and the Community that I was in touch with. Another man might perhaps have been satisfied with the evidence of a purely spiritual bond; I wanted that too, of course, but I also wanted a real historical link. So I always asked these pastors and preachers, at the end of our talks, a question which to them was probably quite unimportant: "When was your Church founded?" The reply usually named the eighteenth, nineteenth or even twentieth century. On hearing that, I felt less surprised that its teaching should not seem entirely the same as Christ's or that of the early Christians.

I usually felt much more at home with the clergy of the leading Protestant Churches—the Lutherans, Anglicans and Calvinists. They were all men of wide and profound culture Many of them knew their Hegel well, and Bergson, and even Marx. Any talk with them soon took on a greater depth, if only because we both spoke the same language. As I myself came from a vaguely Protestant background, I had a feeling that their words stirred memories within me, touched on matters of which I was not wholly ignorant.

Yet Protestantism in all its forms did not quite correspond to what

I was looking for in Christianity. The clergy could not, any more than could the preachers of the sects, convince me of the continuity between primitive Christianity and their Churches. I had the impression that they found my insistence on the point hard to understand. The too purely nationalist structure of all these Churches seemed to lead to lack of universality. Here again they talked a great deal about piety and salvation, but seemed little concerned over the problem, all-important in my eyes, of the temporal salvation of mankind as a whole. I was not, of course, well enough up in religious problems to understand the real values of the Protestant communities. The clergy, for their part, did not seem to try hard enough to explain spiritual realities in relation to my psychological needs.

It is to them, none the less, that I owe my introduction to the Old Testament. I had already glanced at it, but its narratives had seemed to me quite incomprehensible, and I did not see what interest it could have for the people of our day. Then a young Lutheran pastor showed me the continuity between the two Testaments, and pointed out the enduring element of the Old. He had an especially strong admiration for the Prophets, and taught me so to read them that they no longer seemed out-of-date.

A CHURCH TO THE STATURE OF MANKIND

In spite of my utmost efforts and good will, I had not found among Christians what I was looking for. I was beginning to feel discouraged and to tell myself that once again I had been too quick to believe that some solid reality necessarily lay behind what one read in books. Then it was that chance—or, if one prefers it, Providence—put me in touch with a Catholic priest of quite exceptional quality. I know now that most priests are far from coming up to the standard of this famous Jesuit theologian, and that the concept of religion that most of them would have given me would not have been much less narrow than that which I had already picked up among the sects.

The very first day I met this priest, we had a long and profound conversation. He was a masterly dialectician, with a range of culture at least equal to what I had once so greatly admired in the left-wing humanists. It did not take him long to read the state of my soul—he was a subtle psychologist on top of everything else—and decide on the best angle from which to show me the mysteries of the Christian faith.

I learnt, with a great sense of relief, that the Catholic Church attributes at least as much importance as I did myself to its unbroken continuity with the Church that Christ founded in Palestine two thousand years ago. Moreover, the priest told me that the Pope of Rome was the true successor of the Apostle Peter, and that the bishops are the successors of the apostles No one has the right to speak in Christ's name unless he has been given a mandate to share in the mission entrusted by Our Lord to His first disciples. Although he was far from denying the direct action of God—the "Holy Ghost," to use his own term—the priest insisted on the institutional character of the Church. This might have put some people off. But I was as yet unable to understand any mystical action, as such, and here felt myself on firm ground, in an atmosphere where such matters were taken seriously. I should have found it hard, if not impossible, to form an independent judgment of the truth of any given interpretation of Christ's teaching; and it was comforting to learn that there was a Church, founded by Christ Himself, whose task it was to safeguard this teaching and hand it on Everything, of course, depended on the credibility of the Church's claims; the priest promised to give me proofs of it.

Although I had a very good knowledge of Greek, it had never occurred to me to ask myself the etymology of the word "Catholic," and I was surprised and delighted when the priest pointed out that it meant "universal." Indeed, he gave the word an incomparably wider and deeper significance than even the internationalism which had been my own interpretation of it. There could not possibly be a *national* Christian Church, for the Church necessarily embraces all men of all times—and even those who no longer exist in time. I do not think he was exaggerating his real thought for the sake of winning me over. The books he was later to write all set forth this universalist and cosmic concept of Christianity and stressed its essentially communal character. If he did resort to any tactics at this first meeting, they amounted only to this: he did not tell me that not all Catholics—let alone all priests—are as concerned as he with the universalism of the Church: that there are sectarians and individualists, even among Catholics. Like the good teacher he was, he thought it wise to withhold these facts until I was better able to understand them. I see now that he acted throughout with complete loyalty.

For several weeks I spent two or three hours every day in the priest's very modest little cell. The most remarkable feature of this remarkable man was his scrupulous respect for my freedom. I am quite sure that if he had made the least attempt to "convert" or indoctrinate me, I should never have been converted at all. He was far too good a psychologist to provoke my unconscious to a resistance which might hinder what, no doubt, he already saw as the beginning of the work of grace. Right up to the last, he never swerved from the attitude of "scientific" objectivity which he had adopted on the first day. It was never he who took the initiative in deciding what we should talk about: he would speak of the rain or sunshine, ask me about Soviet Russia, the exact meaning of some Marxist term, or something of that sort. I could not help admiring his complete absence of any *a priori* prejudice against Communism. He even got me to moderate my own bitterness, born of such cruel disappointment.

It was always I who embarked on religious topics. Every day I used to note down my thoughts and impressions on what I had just been reading. Whenever I brought up some problem, he always made it a point of honour to answer with the greatest possible intellectual honesty, without any attempt at evasion. He had an astonishing knowledge of history, both sacred and profane; of philosophy, classical and modern literature, and even political economy. His prestige as an intellectual no doubt did much to make me take to him, and to look on myself as his disciple. With him, I never wanted to argue over words or show off how much I knew and what a critical mind I had, as I had always done with the preachers of the various sects.

Our first talks were spent in discussing the social teaching of the Church. It came to me as a startling realization that I, like all the "comrades" alongside whom I'd been living and fighting, had never even known that such teaching existed. I had always thought that the Church was on the side of the established order, upheld the principle of private property, and was the sworn enemy of all social progress. The priest lent me the encyclicals of Leo XIII and Pius XI, and works by various Catholic sociologists of extremely daring outlook.

My *guru* explained, very frankly, why the communism of the early Christians had come to grief. The pooling of all their possessions had seemed to them a logical consequence of Our Lord's command, "Love one another, as I have loved you." But as they believed that they had not long to wait for His Second Coming, and with it the end of the world, there seemed no reason for them to organize their communities with a view to production; they merely put to communal use whatever each one had owned. But community life had always remained the ideal of all Christians aiming at evangelical perfection— and here the priest told me something of monasteries and convents. He said, too, that it was a cause of deep sorrow to him that nearly all Christians who were really trying to lead the life of the Gospels should, for so long, have cut themselves off from the rest of the world. He was delighted at the growing tendency among the best of the Catholic laity to live a communal life; and described the work of several pioneers in this field—Emmanuel Mounier in particular, whom I had met when we were both students.

I had always thought that Karl Marx was the first person to take any real interest in the fate of the working class, which had suffered so greatly from the Industrial Revolution and been so shamelessly exploited by the capitalists. I had never heard of Mgr. von Ketteler, the Bishop of Mayence, who, in the very year of the *Communist Manifesto,* had carried on a fearless campaign for what we know today as a just wage, and for the human dignity of the worker. Then came the birth of social Catholicism—the day of Albert de Mun, the Marquis de la Tour Du Pin, and the Fribourg Conference. A Prince of the Church—Cardinal Manning, Archbishop of Westminster—publicly took his stand on the side of the London dockers when they came out on strike. These are matters which, outside Christian circles, are almost wholly unknown; and no one knows less about them than the Communists.

I read the encyclicals *Rerum Novarum* and *Quadragesimo Anno* with intense interest, and found that the claim for a just wage, and the condemnation of inhuman capitalism, were not the work of a few isolated Christians, but part of the official teaching of the Church.

I told the priest that this discovery came as a flat contradiction of the notion, which I too had always held, that the Church was a stronghold of reaction. In reply, he handed me some mimeographed sheets, containing the most important pronouncements on social questions made by Doctors and Fathers of the Church, and I learnt that St. Basil, St. Gregory of Nyssa, St. Ambrose, and St. Thomas Aquinas himself, had all held the most radical ideas. I will here do no more than quote one passage from the great Bishop of Milan to whom St. Augustine owed his conversion: "The Lord willed that this earth should be owned in common by all men and that its fruits should be for all. It was avarice which gave rise to the rights of property." St. Thomas, less of a preacher and more of a teacher than the Fathers of the Church, saw that private property was better suited to the psychology of men burdened with original sin. But this was only another way of saying that the ideal was collective ownership. And, above all, the great Doctor of the Church stressed the social duties which go hand in hand with the rights of private property. So strongly, in fact, did he insist on this that I drew the perfectly sincere conclusion that capitalist ownership, which had not recognized *any* duties as corresponding to the rights of property, was not covered by his argument When I told the priest that I had reached this conclusion, he showed me the words of Pius XI: "The system of private property is no more absolutely immutable than any other human institution, and history shows it." That was all I needed: I knew now that Christianity was not, in essence, reactionary.

A GLIMPSE OF THE TRANSCENDENT

It was impossible to read Christian books for weeks on end, and to talk every day with a priest, without beginning to see that Christianity is not solely, or even principally, a doctrine of social organization, like Marxism or liberal capitalism. Very gently, the priest opened my eyes to the fact that the Christian concept of community life, as it relates to property and the State, is not just the outcome of ordinary human piety, or of theoretical speculations on economics and the forces of production. No: it has its roots in a fundamental doctrine of Christianity—the doctrine of the Mystical Body and the Communion of Saints.

We read together certain passages of the Gospels, the Acts, and, above all, of St. Paul's Epistles. They dispelled my last doubts: individualism, seen in the light of traditional Christianity, was an utter paradox. But it was no less obvious that the respect for the human person characteristic of Christianity was based on the mystical brotherhood between the Son of God and Mankind which the Incarnation had brought into being Before He left them, Our Lord commanded His disciples to be "one," as He and the Father are One. This, then, was the inspiration of what I knew as Christian communism.

The priest made use of it to introduce me, very briefly, to the Mystery of the Blessed Trinity. The Father, the Son and the Holy Ghost are three distinct Persons, yet They have everything in common, both as to substance and activity. Men could not be "imitators" of God, as Christ Himself told them it was their duty to be, unless they scrupulously respected the likeness of God in themselves and others—*all* others. But how can one be in the image and likeness of God save by realizing, as well as human beings can realize it, the perfect union of the Three Persons within the Godhead? Mankind will never realize all its potentialities or achieve true spiritual maturity until it unites in one great Body, whose members hold everything in common The priest pointed out that it was not just a question of pooling material goods—which don't amount to so very much, after all—but of sharing spiritual riches. It is in this sense alone that Christians can talk of the Mystical Body and the Communion of Saints.

THE FOLLOWING OF CHRIST

The light which my spiritual guide had thrown on the Christian mysteries gave me an almost dazzled sense of exaltation, and my one wish was to find out more. He fell in with this readily enough, and told me that the time had now come for me to start reading books which would teach me the essentials. He was not thinking of text-books on theology. I have already spoken, more than once, of his skill as a psychologist. He knew very well that, in dealing with a conceited young intellectual like myself, one should never begin with an exposition of doctrine and theory, for an intellectual is harder than most people to convince by rational argument. I knew all too many systems and theories already, and if Christian theories had been added to them, I should simply have compared or opposed them to the others—all, apparently, quite as logical. The first thing to aim at was conversion of heart; theories would come later, to reinforce the reasons of the heart with those of the intellect.

When the time was ripe to pass from sociology and history to religion proper, my priest friend lent me the Life of St. Francis of Assisi by Joergensen, the Danish socialist writer and journalist, who was a Catholic convert. I could not, of course, fail to be moved by the sublime poetry of the Poverello's life. My first feeling about it was regret that no such selflessness, no such love for men and all creation, inspired the leaders of Communism. If, in addition to the immense power put at their disposal by modern technical methods and the natural resources of Russia, they had also had the spirit of St. Francis, they might have made a paradise on earth. St. Francis's life showed me that what Communists lacked was love. Their solidarity was a very excellent thing, certainly, but it was strictly limited to Party members; anyone who thought or acted otherwise was outside the pale. Looked at more closely, solidarity as they practised it owed more to self-love than to love.

Somewhat later on, I came to see that there was another great difference between Communism and Christianity. (Here, of course, I am only speaking of the human, psychological side, for where the two teachings are concerned, no comparison is possible.) Christians ask a great deal of the private lives of their leaders; they are expected to be generous and poor, and to do their utmost to follow the example of Christ and the saints. Christians have no very high opinion of Communist leaders who live in magnificent houses and drive about in American cars, and whose wives buy their clothes from famous fashion houses. It all seems to them a betrayal of the impoverished workers for whom the leaders claim to be fighting. But they are forgetting that Communist ethics are not based on an interior life, but on materialism. Militant working-class Communists, when they are cut off from all Christian thought, usually think it quite natural that their leaders should seize all the material advantages open to them. St. Francis in no way embodies the ideals of Marxist-Leninism: if certain Communists do admire him, it is simply because their unconscious is still affected by atavistic complexes derived from Christianity. Both Communists and Christians, no doubt, sigh, with equal longing, for a new world, and dream of a future when men will be better than they are today. The difference between them—and it is a big one—is that Communists think this can be brought about by changing the economic and social structure, whereas Christians—although they do not underestimate or overlook the economic and social side of life—concentrate first and foremost on working an inner transformation of man himself. I did not then know that the Christian method contained as many pitfalls as the Communist. If Communists too often ignore the living man for the sake of an abstract economic order, Christians on their side are too apt to forget how greatly man is conditioned by his economic and political background, which has the fearful power of putting all spiritual freedom out of the reach of a large section of humanity. But this is another story.

After the life of St. Francis came the Lives of Ignatius Loyola,

Francis Xavier, Dominic, Benedict and Charles de Foucauld. The last-named showed me that heroic sanctity is not just a thing of the Christian past; here, at the beginning of our century, so proud of its rationalism and so deeply in thrall to matter, was a cultured man, a man who had known life, yet who lived, down to the smallest detail, like one of the Desert Fathers. A far less perceptive person than my *guru* would have seen that in me he was dealing with an extrovert, a hyperactive. The contemplative saints, leading lives of prayer and penance behind high convent walls, left me comparatively cold; I could not understand them. The Lives of St. Thérèse of Lisieux, Angela of Foligno and Aloysius Gonzaga awoke no answering chord in me. I liked saints who *did* things—went out as missionaries, founded Religious Orders, became social apostles. The only "mere" contemplative whom I admired was Charles de Foucauld. But, as one saw from that period of his life when he was an officer and explorer, he was in fact a man of action who, for reasons which I could not as yet follow, thought it his duty to give up the active life and turn hermit in the heart of the Sahara. I was to learn later that he never ceased to be a man of action, even in the heart of the Sahara.

THE BIRTH OF A NEW MAN

One day I announced to my priest that I wanted to become a Jesuit like St. Ignatius Loyola, Francis Xavier and himself. To me, this request was all the more charged with significance in that I was well aware of the pejorative meaning attached to the word "Jesuit," especially among students: it stood for a hypocrite, a false friend, and an informer. In Soviet Russia, the government and the Party were convinced that there were Jesuits among the saboteurs and spies whom capitalist imperialists were supposed to smuggle into the home of socialism. Far-fetched and horrific stories were told in whispers about the goings-on of these Jesuits. And, lo and behold, the first flesh-and-blood Jesuit I had ever met turned out to be a most remarkable man, a person of great integrity, and a lover of peace and freedom!

I felt extremely surprised, later on, that the priest hadn't burst out laughing at my request. After a few minutes of silence—spent, no doubt, in prayer—he said, very seriously and kindly: "It is by no means impossible. It will need prayer and thought. But have you realized that, if you want to become a Jesuit, you will first have to be a Catholic?"

In fact, I hadn't thought of that. But as it appeared to be the only way of becoming a Jesuit, there seemed no point in refusing the preliminary conditions. I said as much to the priest, and it was agreed that my instruction in the catechism should begin at once; for, as usual, I was in a hurry.

My catechist often showed some surprise at my almost total lack of any difficulties of the purely intellectual order. The Gospel miracles which, right at the beginning, had rather worried me, were no longer a serious obstacle. The same held good as regards the Incarnation, the Virgin Birth, the Redemption, the Blessed Trinity and all the rest. I think on consideration that the reason for this was that I didn't attach much importance to it all. I had turned to Christianity in the hopes of finding there the secret of an intense, authentic life. The Gospels and the saints' biographies had shown me the extraordinary beauty of lives really lived in accordance with the teaching and example of Christ. Remarkable men like Francis, Ignatius, Xavier and de Foucauld (not to mention the apostles and disciples) had believed in the divinity of Christ: what arguments had I to urge against them? I was not looking for new theories, but for reasons for living. These I had found in the lives of Christ's disciples, and I should have thought it pretty childish to quibble over every article of their faith. So I accepted wholesale all that had been their source of inspiration—all that lay behind their wonderful work.

On the evening of August 14th, on my knees before the altar, I recited the solemn abjuration of all heresy and errors of which I might have been guilty, and made my profession of Catholic faith. I was then given conditional baptism, for I did not know whether I had been validly baptized in infancy.

My catechist had done his duty and warned me that I must not expect to feel any sensible effects from either my baptism or my Communion. He tried to make me grasp the reality of their metaphysical efficacy, which does not exclude feeling, but does not postulate it either. None the less, I hoped to see in myself some marks of the transformation that baptism was about to work in my soul. As I was on the point of becoming a "new man," there must surely, I thought, be something to show for it. But alas, the very most I felt was some slight emotion at the actual moment when the waters of baptism touched my forehead. When I left the chapel, there seemed no great change in my feelings about people and things, or my reactions to them. I certainly tried to be more on my guard with any pretty women I met, but I couldn't help knowing that even that resolution was something imposed from without; there was no impulse within me to second it. However, I made up my mind to live, at least for some weeks, on a diet of exclusively holy things—daily Communion, weekly confession, and spiritual books as my sole reading.

What came hardest to me was, of course, confession. At that time I had a very formalist conception of sin. Instead of agreeing with Kierkegaard that the moment a man faces God, he sees himself as a sinner, I thought of sin only as a material act opposed to the Law. Legalism, or even legality, was a value that I had not yet quite assimilated.

As it would have embarrassed me to confess to the priest who knew me so well (in any case, I was about to leave the town where he lived), I used to make my confessions to priests whom I chose at random. They, of course, did not know anything about me, and generally treated me as if I had been a practising Catholic all my life. They too referred everything to the Law and the Commandments, and their words seldom awoke any responsive echo in my soul. The result was that, at this stage, my religious life was cast in a somewhat narrow and formalistic mould. I judged other Christians with quite inhuman severity, the slightest discrepancy between their conduct and the teaching of the Gospels used to call forth astonishingly uncharitable criticism. I subjected myself to rigid asceticism, in which there was much less piety than pride. The confessors to whom I went made the mistake of talking too much of the sins of the flesh, almost never of the sins of the spirit. They did, it's true, speak of humility, but it was the humility of the pharisee jockeying for position with the publican. This experience was useful to me later: it showed me how seriously a Christian's spiritual life may suffer if he does not happen to hit on an intelligent and experienced guide. If priests only had in them a little more of the *guru* and a little less of the judge, it would be an unmixed blessing to the Church and human souls.

Nevertheless, sketchy though my religious education had been before my baptism, and superficial though my knowledge was of Christian spirituality, I was, beyond question, from the day of my baptism, firmly anchored in the faith. Although I hardly knew how to pray, had little idea of the demands of Christian living, and did not feel any inner force driving me towards it, grace had none the less begun its work in me. Many years have passed since my baptism, during which time—as happens with all Christians—periods of great fervour have alternated with periods of aridity and painful disillusionment; yet I see it as a special grace that I have never suffered from doubts or difficulties in matters of faith. True, I have had to face serious difficulties within the Church, I have known moments of discouragement and hesitation, but never once was faith itself involved.

The story of my conversion, as I have so far related it, is a pure piece of phenomenology. Psychological happenings are not, of course, a sufficient cause for conversion, for the bonds between God and man, which conversion tightens, touch that part of the soul which eludes all psychological investigation. In the last analysis, conversion is always the work of God alone. It is only through barely perceptible signs that man becomes aware of the profound but always secret action of God's grace within him. As to describing it with anything approaching accuracy, that is out of the question. St. Augustine himself only partly succeeded in doing so. How can one explain why God chose to make His voice heard at that stage of my life and not another? Was it really the first time that grace had sought me out? Why had I not felt its touch until after I had spent so many years search-

ing for truth outside God? I could, of course, answer these questions
—and many others—by more or less plausible hypotheses. The only
aspect of my conversion of which I can give an exact phenomenological description is its purely human, psychological and sociological context. I had been bitterly disappointed in Communism, and had had a
short but extremely unsatisfying taste of an aimless existence; there
was clearly a void within me, which God saw fit to fill. The books I
read, the men I met, would probably have meant nothing to me if I
had come across them some months earlier.

Any attempt to establish a link of strict cause and effect between
despair and disillusionment on the one hand, and conversion on the
other, would certainly lead me wide of the mark. Yet, as I have seen
in my own case and the case of many other people, if God's grace is to
do its work of making a new man, man himself must be in a state of
"disposability" and anxious speculation. Grace nearly always knocks
in vain at the doors of a satisfied heart; the knocking goes unheard.
It matters little whether the satisfaction is material, intellectual or
affective.

MONASTERIES AND CONVENTS

I had wanted to become a Jesuit. The General of the Society of
Jesus, to whom I was recommended, showed me great kindness and
understanding, but let me see that the time had not come to take so
serious a step. I had seen nothing of the Christian world: I knew the
Church only through the eyes of a Jesuit. The General estimated
that I should need at least three years before I could make any such
self-commitment with full knowledge of what I was doing. It took
me a long time to see how wise his advice was. It is a pity that some
other religious orders, which have too strong a dash of the recruiting
sergeant in their composition, do not always show an equal caution.
Many mistakes would be avoided if they did.

Backed by the priest who had introduced me to Christianity, and
the support of various lay Catholics whom I had come to know, I
decided to begin my apprenticeship to the Christian world straight

away. My best way of doing so would no doubt have been to find some post as a teacher, play my part in parish affairs as an ordinary parishioner, and finally take up some form of Catholic Action. Had I done so, I should have come to meet Christians in their own setting of family and social life. Instead of this, I set out on a tour of monasteries and convents.

So, once again, I let myself be led by my "temperament," running instinctively to extremes—to the absolute. I had already experienced the serious disadvantages of doing so, but also (let me admit it) certain advantages, the chief of which was that I had always lived with great intensity. No sooner had I joined the Young Communists than I became a keen militant, and—not long after—a professional revolutionary. And the same sort of process was now being repeated in my Catholic life. It was not until many years later, when I had lost much of the impulsiveness and spontaneity of youth, that I began to ask myself if I should not have been better advised to lead an ordinary Christian life. But at the time it never even occurred to me to wonder. I was now a Christian, and it seemed to follow as a logical consequence that I should enlist forthwith in the army of militants—the religious orders and the priesthood in general I never even asked myself if I had the qualities necessary for the religious life, or whether my past way of living might have left me no very fit subject for what I knew to be a state of perfection. For, as I saw it, neither the religious life nor the priesthood had as its main object the personal perfection of those who embraced it. I regarded both, somewhat too exclusively, as armies of fighters.

After the Jesuits, the first Order which I came to know was that of St. Francis. This was due partly to the deep admiration I felt for the Poverello after reading Joergensen's book, and partly to more or less fortuitous circumstances.

The Father Guardian of the Friary at Antwerp in Belgium gave me a welcome which I felt was in the best traditions of the *Fioretti*. The Father Superior was young and very dynamic—even exuberant; he was also an extremely cultured man, who had just published a remarkable book on the Franciscan thinker, Roger Bacon. Was it just

my inexperience, or was there really some deliberate contrivance in it
all? Whatever the answer, the two days I spent with the Franciscans
gave me an impression of great spontaneity and freedom in the religious life. The Father Superior and some of the young, highly educated Friars used to sit up with me till late at night, discussing philosophy, literature and politics over tankards of beer. I felt that St.
Francis would have been pleased with his sons.

In reality—as I found when I had visited several other Franciscan
houses—the atmosphere which so struck me at Antwerp was due
partly to the exceptional personality of the Father Guardian, but still
more to the fact that he had thought it advisable to introduce me to
the more "Franciscan" side of his Order. Some days later I was the
guest of the Franciscan Friary at Mons, the headquarters of the
scholastics. Here I found that the sons of St. Francis lived under a
strict and fairly complicated set of rules, and that the charming fan-
tasies of the early days were a mere memory. I was allowed to have my
meals in the refectory and take part in the Office, and I thought it
all very interesting; but it was a disappointment to find, so far as I
could judge, little trace left of original Franciscanism.

WITH THE MONKS

It was at the Abbey of Maredsous in Belgium that I first met the
Benedictines. I was deeply impressed by the monastery, which is
perched on a fairly high mountain, in the midst of magnificent scenery; and I could not fail to be touched by the simple, cordial Benedictine hospitality, which so exactly expressed my idea of Christian
charity. I had already, once or twice, come across the distrust of
strangers which characterizes certain "middle-class-ified" priests; in
fact, I had even met with it in some religious communities. But here
a guest could really feel himself a messenger from God.

At Maredsous the Divine Office was invested with a solemnity
that went far beyond anything I had seen among the Franciscans,
Redemptorists and certain other "active" orders. Unfortunately, I

still didn't know much about the glories of the liturgy, which I looked at from the purely aesthetic point of view.

What impressed me more than anything was the serene joy and deep peace which radiated from all the monks. I had several long talks with a very old lay brother who had been at Maredsous for more than sixty years, and was now no longer strong enough to play a useful part in community life, except by looking after the farmyard. The way he talked about his long life as a lay brother showed me beyond all possible doubt what deep happiness it had given him. He took me to see the Abbey graveyard; I was quite surprised by its lovely simplicity—surprised, too, to find, from the tablets on the wooden crosses, how extraordinarily long-lived the monks were. I read, for instance, that Brother So-and-So had died at the age of eighty or ninety, after spending fifty, or perhaps seventy, years at Maredsous. As is the custom in Benedictine monasteries, I shared the life of the monks in every detail, in refectory and chapel, and saw for myself that it made few concessions to comfort or laziness.

The day after I came to Maredsous I felt a strong wish never to leave it, and asked the Father Abbot if I might extend my stay, that I might get to know the life better. But it is only half of my nature which has always longed for a quiet life and would gladly give itself up to learning or solitude. Before I had been long at Maredsous I saw that I should never be able to spend my whole life praying and singing the praises of the Lord. The choir monks did indeed devote several hours a day to intellectual work, but it was work of scholarship for which I knew I was quite unfitted. I had too passionate a love for the world, with all its excitements and disappointments, to be able to give it up finally and fundamentally. At the end of about a week I came down from the Mount Tabor that Maredsous had been to me. Perhaps I was wrong. Perhaps it would have been better if I had forced myself to break with the world. Certainly, ever since that short stay, it has always been a joy to me to spend a few days, from time to time, at a Benedictine abbey. But, as on this first occasion, my need to go back to the world will take no denial after a very short time there.

At the Trappist monastery of Notre Dame du Désert in Languedoc I had the joy of attending the funeral of the Father Abbot. I say "the joy" deliberately, for never, before or since, have I had so piercing a certainty of the reality of eternal life. A superhuman joy shone in the faces of all the monks, who had loved the Father Abbot as if they were his sons. They "knew," with a conviction that went far beyond any mere mathematical certainty, that their Father had at last won the reward of his long life of penance and mystical love. The Guest Master explained to me after the ceremony that to a Trappist the day of mourning and burial (burial of the "old man") is the day when he enters the monastery, for this implies the complete renunciation of the whole world. Death itself is seen only as rebirth to true life.

Yet I felt that I was even less fitted to join the Trappists than to enter the Benedictine order. In the case of the Benedictines, the life of silence and asceticism does not imply a complete renunciation of the human: it still has all the aesthetic values of the liturgy, and an intense intellectual activity. There is less of this among the Trappists, in Europe, at least. Most of the Trappist monasteries which I visited at about that time seemed to be under a blight of gloomy ugliness. The Office in choir was deliberately stripped of everything which could afford pleasure to an aesthete, and nowhere did I see any of the wonderful libraries which had made my mouth water in Benedictine monasteries. But what to me seemed hardest of all was the obligation of keeping silence, without any possibility of retiring to the solitude and intimacy of one's cell. All that the Trappist has, at night, is a kind of box in the communal dormitory. By day he has to live and work among the other monks without ever being allowed to say a single word to them. And, to crown it all, those I observed seemed to attach almost no importance to the most rudimentary laws of cleanliness.

Taking it all round, and supposing that my need for human sociability had not been as overpowering as it was, the monastery which I should have preferred above all others was the Chartreuse. The loveliest of them all—the Grande Chartreuse—I did not see until after the war: in 1936 it was still uninhabited. But I spent a memorable day at the Chartreuse of Montrieux, in Provence. Life there was perhaps even more austere than among the Trappists. But the fact that each monk had a small house of his own, and that the rule allowed intellectual work, seemed to me to make his conditions more human. (Some people may consider this a terrible imperfection on my part, but I must confess that I have never regarded—and do not now regard—Christian perfection as the negation of the human, but rather as its fulfilment.)

Like many other people, I had always thought that the Benedictine, Trappist and Carthusian abbeys were exclusively the refuge of men who had been disappointed or defeated by life. Great was my surprise when I discovered, at Montrieux on that occasion and, later, at the Grande Chartreuse—and, of course, at all other monasteries of strict observance—that almost all the men who tried to enter them were young, strong and well-balanced. I learnt, moreover, that the Carthusians hold that those best fitted for the eremitical life are light-hearted young men, optimistic and even high-spirited. The plaster saint type that people in the world are apt to associate with the "mystics" is almost always refused the habit. A Chartreuse—or, for the matter of that, any other monastery—has no use for a neurotic. Only extremely well-balanced men of great vitality can hope to strike roots in the austere silence.

THE DOMINICANS OF JUVISY AND ELSEWHERE

A hitch on the railway was the reason for my getting to know the Dominicans better than any other religious order. Some friends had told me about the Dominicans of Juvisy near Paris, and the extraordinary man—Père Bernadot—who was their animating spirit. I was invited to spend a few days in this hive of intense intellectual activity, where *La Vie Spirituelle* and *La Vie Intellectuelle* were published. The titles of these periodicals show their scope, but give no real idea of the broadmindedness, the extraordinary gift for entering into every form of anguish that besets man today, which distinguished their editors, both lay and clerical. A third review, *Sept,* filled me with even greater admiration. It, too, was directed by Père Bernadot, and was probably the most fearless attempt made by French Catholics to break down the walls of the ghetto behind which so many of them had retreated. The editors of *Sept* were committed, up to the hilt, to the fight for social justice; they sought, wholeheartedly and intelligently, every opportunity for discussion with anyone who seemed really to have the good of the people at heart. If necessary, they did not hesitate to take up positions directly opposed to the time-honoured prejudices of Catholic society. They spoke out in favour of the French Popular Front, and denounced the cause of Franco in Spain.

My stay at Juvisy left me with one particularly precious memory, for it was there that I had the good fortune to meet Joseph Folliet, whose friendship has never since failed me. Père Bernadot announced one day that we were going to dine with the "chief editor of *Sept,* Joseph Folliet, one of the most famous leaders of progressive French Catholicism"; and that it would be greatly to my advantage to know him.

He was a fat man, who looked as if he did himself very well—not at all my idea of a Catholic leader. He entertained us with endless funny stories and songs of his own invention, and only took his pipe out of his mouth to swallow a mouthful of food or a draught of wine. I found it hard to understand how anyone could be both a dauntless fighter for truth and a complete humanist—using the word in more or less the sense it bore during the Renaissance. I was later to be grateful to him for the lesson he unconsciously gave me that day.

As I soon found out, the Dominicans of Juvisy were by no means typical of their Order in the twentieth century. Some time later, for example, I found myself at Saint-Maximin, the stronghold of uncompromising Thomism, the headquarters of the *Revue Thomiste.* It was all far too reminiscent of Communist intellectual authoritarianism; and that, however sugar-coated, and in however good a cause, was henceforth always to be hateful for me.

AT THE S. U.

"S.U." is the name affectionately given, by its masters and their students, to the Seminaire Universitaire of Lyons. It stands perched on the hillside of Fourvière, which swarms with churches and religious houses. Once again it was chance—the non-religious man's word for Providence—which made me a student of the Theological Faculty of the Catholic University in Lyons, whose students lived in the S.U. None of the religious communities that I had so far seen suited me so well as this seminary, where spiritual fervour, intellectual enthusiasm, and the glorious liberty of the children of God, lived in harmony side by side.

Among the professors of the Theological Faculty—many of them quite outstanding men—was Père Henri de Lubac, who stood head and shoulders above any of the innumerable teachers it has ever been my lot to listen to. He soon acquired a decisive influence over the whole trend of my Christian life and methods of intellectual inquiry. I had read his theological masterpiece, *Catholicisme,* with breathless interest, as soon as it came out. I still think that Père de Lubac has written the best of all syntheses of Christianity, a synthesis which is both completely faithful to the original inspiration of the Christian faith, and perfectly designed to meet the educated man's needs of heart and mind in our own day. Few thinkers have ever shown so clearly the bond between the eternal and the actual.

Père de Lubac's course of lectures on the main trends of spiritual life was certainly remarkable for its erudition, but to me it was, above all else, a lesson in the difficult art of intellectual charity. Up to that time, I had often been shocked by the way in which Christian theologians and philosophers "liquidated" everyone whose opinions did not exactly coincide with their own. In a certain famous theological school I have heard some of the professors—models of charity in every other way—oversimplifying, with staggering intellectual dishonesty, the philosophy of such men as Kant and Descartes, just for the fun of making them look ridiculous in the eyes of their young students. Even Catholic theologians and philosophers were referred to contemptuously, if they belonged to some other school of thought. It was not easy to see the difference between such methods and those current in the Soviet Union, which I have described in an earlier chapter.

There was none of all this in Père de Lubac. He would never have dreamed, for the sake of facile—and inevitably unsuccessful—apologetics, of slurring over the smallest detail of whatever it was which gave the system he was describing its inner strength. He would speak of Buddha, Luther, Proudhon, Nietzsche, with so much feeling: he took such pleasure in pointing out to us all that was true and beautiful in their work, that anybody unaware of the real state of affairs might well have thought himself at the lecture of a Buddhist or a Proudhon-ite And when at last he came to the summing-up of the systems and theories which he had outlined with such scrupulous fairness, he showed no trace of the malicious delight with which sectarian minds "refute" their opponents. Quite clearly, it grieved him that thinkers who in many ways were so powerful and likable should make these mistakes. It was Henri de Lubac who showed me that the notion of catholicity can apply even to one's intellectual behaviour.

Our teacher of dogma, Père Louis Richard, had an equally undogmatic mind. He did his best to keep to his schedule, but his intellectual—one may say, his forceful—temperament broke through all the restrictions and routine methods imposed by pseudo-tradition. His teaching didn't conform much to the textbooks, but it had the enormous advantage of giving us an appetite for theology. When we left the lecture hall, we hardly ever felt the sense of relief which usually fills students when they can tell themselves, "Well, that's another one over." Instead, we used to make a rush for the library, to look out the best writings of the Fathers of the Church and contemporary thinkers. As a general rule, the teaching given in seminaries so puts off theological students that very few priests, even among the young intellectuals, ever again open a book on theology: but almost all of Père Richard's many past students have retained their liking for this form of discipline.

The cult of the Bible and the Fathers of the Church was undoubtedly the distinctive feature of the Lyons Theological Faculty. I myself owe another debt to Père Richard: it was he who introduced me to the inner history of French Catholicism. He told me the wonderful story of the Sillon movement which had fired his own youth and whose guiding principle still meant much to him. From him, too, I learnt how the liberty of the children of God had been successively threatened by Maurrassism, Integrism, the "Sapinière," and so on. It is not surprising that the masters of the S. U. should have been among the first victims of the Integrist revenge in the '50's.

The head of the S. U., Père Girard, was in no sense an intellectual: in fact, he was really a contrast to the prevailing spirit of the house. But he was, in the best sense of the term, a man with a heart. There were at the seminary a certain number of young men who had gone there straight from their secondary schools; but there were also many men of thirty and over—former teachers, lawyers, journalists, engineers, officers, doctors. Père Girard instinctively and visibly preferred the younger men, who had all the purity and docility which was the keynote of his own personality. Yet none of the older students ever had cause to complain that he showed favouritism. Père Girard accomplished the feat of treating each one of us as an individual, making the fullest possible allowances for our own personal ways and temperaments; and he managed to do so without ever arousing jealousy.

By various small signs I was well aware that, naturally enough, the Superior did not feel particularly drawn towards me. His childhood and youth had been so utterly unlike mine that, on the natural plane, there was nothing to bring us together. Yet I never met with the slightest injustice at his hands. Without going into the question of whether his decision was wise or unwise, both for myself and for the Church, I am certain, now that I know ecclesiastical ways better, that no other head of a seminary would have sent up my name for ordination. For I was strangely ill-adapted to the ecclesiastical state.

What of my sixty fellow students? Most of them, especially the young ones, no doubt felt that I was too unlike them for any friendship to be possible between us. The men I got on best with were those who, like myself, had come late to the study of theology and were in general not much better fitted than I was to seminary life. However, there was never any real friction, and the kindness that everybody showed me is something that I still remember with pleasure. It was only during my last year at the Faculty that there were some fairly unpleasant disagreements. These, however, had nothing to do with the life of the seminary as such: it was simply a matter of Gaullists and Pétainists splitting up into opposite camps.

On our return to the seminary in November 1940 we were all feeling depressed by the defeat of France Most of us had been called up and had some personal experience of the disaster of May and June. We nearly all hoped for great things from the national revolution of the old Marshal, who claimed that he was going to clean up France. Those like myself who had an instinctive revulsion from a government on the Fascist model, kept in power by the victorious Nazis, felt they had lost their bearings, and didn't know which side to take.

Towards the end of December we were joined by two Alsatian seminarists who had just been demobilized. To them the issue was clear-cut. Pétain had handed Alsace over to Hitler and we must therefore stand up to him. Within a few weeks, the S. U. had become one of the first strongholds of active resistance in Lyons. With the tacit connivance of the Superior and directors, our small printing press turned out one of the first "underground" pamphlets. We helped to distribute *La Voix du Vatican*—a clandestine news-letter which came out before *Témoignage chrétien*—and many booklets. The Pétainist clique knew perfectly well what we were up to, but the spirit of solidarity at the S. U. was stronger than any divergence of political opinion.

On June 29th, 1941, in the basilica of Fourvière, the Church raised me to the priesthood through the hands of Cardinal Gerlier.

There are no words to describe the peaceful happiness that was mine that day.

The next morning I said my first Mass in the presence of Père de Lubac and several others of my past teachers. Among the friends who came to receive Communion and my first blessing was dear Emmanuel Mounier, who in my eyes was the living incarnation of the Christian's anguish in the world of today.

When I saw, kneeling before me, people whom I admired and knew to be nearer to God than I was, I suddenly realized that ordination to the priesthood had made me an object of faith to myself. Humanly speaking, I was no better than I had been the day before, and not really very different. But I *knew*, with unshakable certainty, that from now on, at my words, the bread and wine would be changed into the Body and Blood of Christ, and that, through me, God would pour out forgiveness and blessing on mankind.

· I was wrong, of course, to think and hope that from that day forward everything would become clear-cut and simple, and that my life would follow a straight course already marked out for me. The future was soon to show that this was by no means the case. On the contrary: everything still remained to be done.